THE WALK

Memoir of a Liberian Civil War Survivor

BRIMA K. LAMIN
In collaboration with **CHANTALE WESLEY-LAMIN**

WESLEY LAMIN BOOKS
Helping People One Book at a Time
A portion of the proceeds benefit charity

WESLEY LAMIN BOOKS
Helping People One Book at a Time

Published in 2016 by Wesley Lamin Books, L.L.C.

First paperback edition, 2016

Paperback ISBN-13: 978-0-9976379-0-8
Paperback ISBN-10: 0-9976379-0-0

Cover design by Jimmy Gibbs. Map by iStock.com/bogdanserban. Front cover soldier photograph by iStock.com/Sean_Warren. Front cover male model, author's son, Reginald Hardy, Jr. Photographed by Chantale Wesley-Lamin. Back cover photograph of Brima Lamin taken in 1994 at age fifteen. Editing by Ruotolo Agency and Pastor Bill Gibson.

For upcoming releases, book purchases, speaking engagements and other services, please contact:

Wesley Lamin Books, L.L.C.
<u>Email</u>: wesleylaminbooks@gmail.com
<u>Websites</u>: www.wesleylaminbooks.com / www.WLBnc.com

DEDICATION

We give praises and honor to our Almighty God for being the author and finisher of our lives.

This book is dedicated to the best part of us, our children. Jalen, Reginald, Bella and Uriah, you are all wonderfully and uniquely made. Remember to keep God first in your *walk* and everything else will be added unto you.

My war experience began at age eleven. All accounts are based on my recollection of the events that I witnessed. For privacy, some names have been changed. While people are referenced from various religious backgrounds, tribal descents, etc., please know that the actions of some in no way represent an entire group of people.

CONTENTS

ACKNOWLEDGMENTS

From Brima K. Lamin

To my father, Mr. Brima Lamin. Without you, we would have never survived the war. Your love and care kept our family alive. I will forever be grateful.

To my mother, Mrs. Marie Perry Lamin, thank you for your prayers and unconditional love.

My dearest grandmother, Mrs. Edna Toles, thank you for always being there to open up your home and take us in when we had nowhere to go.

To Pastor Alfred Blidi, your teaching gave me the knowledge of Jesus Christ, forever changing my life. Thank you for giving me hope in a time of hopelessness.

I thank all of my siblings, Opa, Francis, Mariama, Opi (late), Curtis, Boakai, Beindu (Edna), and Peter, for all the love that you have shown me over the years.

To my ROTC leaders, Major Jesse Brock and Sergeant Ralph Julian, thank you for giving me courage and teaching me how to believe in myself.

To Mother Liberia, we will rise again! Thank you for making me the man that I am today!

From Chantale Wesley-Lamin

To my parents, Ms. Victoria Wesley and Mr. William Johnson, thank you for putting me before yourselves and for your spoken and unspoken love.

I thank my older brother, Chip, for being the most influential person in my life and for shielding me from the darkness. I love you buddy!

To my Wesley family, I love you all so much! To my beautiful grandmother, Mom Rain, thanks for showing me the strength of a woman. I can only hope that I have made you and the pillars of our family, Grum-Mom Pearl and Grum-Pop Buck, proud!

To my Elias family, I look forward to many years of making up for lost time and for all of the fond memories to come.

To Cher and the members of the Jackson Five+++..., I say thank you for being the epitome of family unity and true unconditional love. RIP King Garry F. Jackson, with love, Your Sweet Tooth!

My dear friend, Mrs. Nicole Johnson, you are truly a virtuous woman! I admire your ability to overcome and thank you for continuously speaking words of encouragement over my life.

I thank all of the wonderful educators that have sown into me over the years. A special thanks to my 8th grade English teacher, Ms. Toki, for telling me that I "could" and "would". I still have the letter that you wrote me all those years ago! To Mr. Thomas Wesley, sir, I thank you for your firm pointer finger and instilling the importance of using proper grammar.

MAP

INTRODUCTION

The struggle for freedom and democracy for Liberia stretches back hundreds of years. Since she originally gained her independence from America on July 26, 1847, Liberia has struggled to find her identity in the world. Some of these struggles happened very early in my days. On April 12, 1980 Samuel K. Doe, a sergeant in the armed forces of Liberia, led a coup d'état against President William R. Tolbert. He became the first native-born Liberian to gain power. He changed the course of history by ending hundreds of years of Americo-Liberian rule. Americo-Liberians were the descendants of freed slaves that returned to Africa after the abolishment of slavery in the United States.

Nearly a decade after President Samuel K. Doe came into power, a new face of politics emerged...or rather an old face, Charles Taylor. Before being removed for embezzlement, Taylor worked in the Liberian government under Doe. After a stint in Libya, he returned to Liberia as the head of the National Patriotic Front of Liberia (NPFL) aiming to overthrow the Doe regime. Taylor waged an open war on December 24, 1989. His decision led to fifteen years of fighting, claiming the lives of over a quarter million Liberians and leaving thousands more, including myself, displaced and seeking refuge in other countries. Many of those committing heinous acts of violence during the war were child soldiers, including some of my own friends and relatives.

The Walk is not just my story, but a story of an entire nation still trying to rise from the ashes of it's past. It exposes what it looks like to be completely stripped of all that you have ever known and still have faith to forge ahead. Through the eyes of me as an adolescent boy, *The*

Walk begs you to question how you will walk in the midst of adversity, trials and triumph.

Let the *walk* begin!

1 D-DAY

This was happening. Not in some far off place or unknown land, but right here in my own neighborhood.

Ask any Liberian what caused the Liberian Civil War and you are bound to get countless answers. Even my own parents differed with ma adamant that the fighting was over rice. Can you imagine people fighting over rice? I can't, but I certainly can understand how the power and greed exercised by one group, in this instance to control rice prices, at the expense of another group can cause division. Pa, on the other hand, said that the war started over tribal division. Within the small country, which is similar in size to the state of Louisiana, there were thirteen counties. These counties were home to some sixteen tribes or people of the same descent. Some tribes were more concentrated in one county versus another. Then there were counties like Montserrado, near the capital where we lived, that had a mixture of tribes. Pa was from the Mende tribe and was born and raised in Sierra Leone, which borders Liberia on the west. He came to Liberia to go to school and met ma, a native of Liberia from the Vai tribe. This tribe also existed in Sierra Leone.

Tribal division was especially evident in the political realm. The President in office, Samuel K. Doe, and most of those in a position of leadership during his tenure were from the Krahn tribe. This did not sit well with many Liberians who felt that this led to economic disparity, imbalance of power and entrenched political corruption. For me, at age eleven, this was all over my head. That is, until December 24, 1989. I sat with my two brothers, Curtis and Boakai, watching the news report about fighting in the countryside. The Liberian television station did not have all day broadcasting, so airing began at 6:00 p.m. with news coverage. We tried to make sense of what we had heard. Fighting between the rebels and government troops…what did all of this mean? Later that night my parents explained that the rebels were people who had turned against the government. We really didn't think much of the news report because it seemed to be an isolated incident, far from where we lived.

We woke up the next morning and it was Christmas day. I was excited because this was one of the few days of the year that we ate chicken. It was somewhat of a delicacy in our house because the chicken feed, which was often imported, was very expensive. Early that morning ma prepared a feast with chicken gravy and rice. We had a great time and even got a visit from "old man beggar". He was a guy that dressed in raggedy clothes with a stuffed potbelly and a silly mask. He danced while his entourage sang and played the sangba drums. Each family in the neighborhood gave them money in exchange for their entertainment. After dinner, my siblings and I were each given a present. While they were not wrapped, it was exciting to receive a gift. The boys usually got toy guns while the girls got dolls. Thereafter, we dressed in our best clothing and joined our friends in walking around the neighborhood showing everything off. These were fun traditions.

On February 11, 1990, the news of Nelson Mandela's release from prison after twenty-seven years of captivity spread all around the world. I remembered learning about his great contributions to end South African apartheid and his subsequent imprisonment. As the announcement echoed over the airways of British Broadcasting Corporation (BBC) Radio, the streets filled with people rejoicing, dancing and shouting, "Freeeeee, Nelson Mandela! Liberia say, freedom we want!" Yet and still, Liberia was not free. In parts of our own country, war raged on and like many South Africans, we were a group of countrymen divided.

Life continued to go as normal. For me, this meant school. I was in the sixth grade attending Saint Kizito Catholic School about three miles from our house. My parents made a decent living, so unlike some other families, we were afforded the opportunity to start school at age five. I was actually the youngest child in my class. Being amongst some students who were fifteen and older, I often hid my age in an effort to fit in.

In Liberia, it was not uncommon to have extended family living under one roof. My parents were giving people who took in relatives and strangers alike. In total there were nine people living in our five-bedroom house. They were my ma and pa, eight-year-old sister Beindu and five adopted brothers. Peter was the youngest at age two, Curtis was eleven like me, Boakai was twelve, Opi was twenty and Opa was twenty-three. I also had an older brother and sister who stayed in neighboring cities. Francis was twenty-one and Mariama was fourteen. Our house, situated on two acres of land surrounded by coconut and mango trees, had just been built five years prior. This was a major accomplishment for my parents who had worked so hard to move us from renting a room in someone else's house to finally having a place of our own. I watched as the concrete blocks morphed into this pristine, white structure with a bright red tin roof. In addition to the bedrooms, inside there was a living room, dining area and kitchen. Tile and concrete floors ran throughout. An attached one-car garage and porch completed the outside. A small breezeway connected the main house to the outdoor bathhouse which included a floor drain and concrete commode connected to an underground septic tank.

By the end of May 1990, pa's relatives fled from Grand Bassa County bringing the total to twenty children and adults living in our house. They gave accounts of brutal acts of violence against civilians by both the rebels and government troops alike. They said that in many cases the rebels captured villages and towns with little resistance. Nevertheless, President Doe reported that we had nothing to worry about so my parents continued to go to work and we went to school as normal.

We lived in Paynesville, which is a suburb east of the capital city of Monrovia. It had several communities clustered together making it geographically larger than the capital. Each community had its own unique name. We lived in Morris' Farm. Within a few miles of our neighborhood, there was the Coca-Cola Factory, the Red Light Market, the largest commercial market district in the country and the Omega Transmitter, the highest structure in Africa. Since our neighborhood was on a direct route to the countryside, we often saw truckloads of government armed forces in long convoys. They were all suited in their green uniforms, armed with assault rifles. It was exciting so we stood alongside the road cheering them on to victory. While most of the trucks returned empty, the news reported that the government troops maintained control, so we were hopeful.

On Monday, July 2, 1990, ma woke up with a bad feeling. For as long as I can remember, she could sense when something was not right. In fact, she had been given the nickname "Joseph the Dreamer" for her premonitions. Before leaving out for work around 7:00 a.m., she warned that we should not go to school. She was a nurse and midwife at John F. Kennedy Medical Center in Monrovia so typically she would not get home until the evening. Pa returned home early that morning from the night shift. He worked as a radio technician at Voice of America (VOA) in Careysburg about fifteen miles from the house. He was dropped off, as usual, by the company van that transported him to and from work. He said that he heard gunfire around his workplace but did not see any fighting. After washing up, he laid down for a nap. A few of my brothers and I decided to go outside for some fresh air. We headed to our favorite spot under the tree on the side of the house.

"Let me beat you!" Opi cockily said as he set up the homemade checkerboard that we had drawn on a piece of cardboard. He was always so darn competitive.

"We will see," I replied, nodding my head and taking my seat on the cinderblock as Curtis and Boakai looked on. I gathered all the Fanta bottle caps as my pieces and gave him the Coca-Cola caps. "Your go."

Opi studied the board like a surgeon then slowly slid his piece diagonally to a black space. I shook my head with annoyance and quickly moved my piece.

BOOOOOMMMMM! Opi slid another one of his caps. "Ya'll hear dat?"

"It tunder," Boakai said, standing over us. I glanced at the sky and it was clear. The sun was up.

"Your go BK," Opi impatiently chimed in.

Brushing it off, I slid my piece again. Opi rubbed his chin in thought and carefully moved his piece in my direction. *He is so predictable*, I thought, as I changed course. We alternated turns a few more times and out of nowhere he jumped me.

"I kill your man!" he boasted. Curtis and Boakai laughed. I couldn't believe that he backdoored me like that. I completely overlooked his other man.

BOOOOOMMMMM!

My eyes shifted and I immediately stood up. "What's dat! Dat not tunder-oh!"

Everyone started laughing at my reaction. "BK, it probably someone trying to start an old car! Your move!"

BOOOOOOOOOOOOOOMMMMMMMMMMMMMM!

A third explosion went off and the ground shook like an earthquake. This time it was followed by what sounded like a long whistle and yet another explosion. Within seconds, we heard continuous gunfire as if someone simultaneously set off hundreds of firecrackers. We all stood there looking at each other in a state of confusion. I wondered if I should run but I stood frozen. Just then, pa came running around the side of the house.

"Ya'll come inside! Come inside!" he screamed, motioning us towards the back door.

Ducking, we ran through the kitchen and into the living room. Everyone else had done the same.

"GET DOWN! On da floor! On da flooooooorrr!" Pa panted as he shoved some of the slow movers down! Immediately, bullets flew through the house, hitting doors and breaking windows. They zipped through so quickly that I knew that it was only a matter of time before one of us got hit. As the glass shattered, all we could do was take cover with our hands over our heads. I could not believe that this was happening. Not in some far off place or unknown land, but right here in my own neighborhood. At that moment, I realized that all the stories we heard about the war were true. We were living it for ourselves.

During the midst of the shooting, pa crawled to the bedroom. When he returned, he had his work identification. He was drenched with sweat.

"Shhhhhhhhhhhhh! Ya'll be quiet! Be quiet! Dere's one of them in the front yard," he whispered.

All nineteen of us laid cramped in the living room with the adults hovering over the children. It felt like a sauna and my heart nearly pounded out of my chest with each passing second. The rampant gunfire continued on for hours and no one spoke a word. It was as if fear crippled my body and I had succumbed to the idea that we would all die. Finally, the shooting stopped. We heard voices outside. People were yelling in Gio, a native language spoken by the Gio tribe from Nimba County. While we heard the language used before by our neighbors, we were not fluent.

Soon a neighbor yelled to pa, "Mr. Lamin, dey want you out da house! Get out da house now!"

The first thing that came to my mind was that they were going to blow up the house. Everyone panicked, ran outside and darted in different directions. Pa snatched Beindu onto his waist and quickly vanished amongst the hundreds of people already scattered about. It was like every man was for himself. I just followed someone...anyone. My adrenaline was so high that I ran for a mile without stopping. Surrounded by strangers, I was relieved to see Curtis. He asked me about the whereabouts of the others, but I explained that I had not seen anyone. We decided to stick with the crowd and run towards the Monrovia-Kakata Highway, which led out of the city. We were in the front of a pack of about one hundred people. As we ran around a curb, we were suddenly met by two men armed with assault rifles.

"Hold it!" they screamed, taking a shooting stance with their rifles pointed directly at us.

We immediately put our hands up in surrender. I felt my heart pounding in my chest and time seemed to stand still. There was no mistake about it. These were the rebel soldiers we heard about. I had always wondered what they would look like. I figured that they would be direct opposites of the government troops. What that would be, I was not exactly sure, but somehow I knew that it had to be scary. They wore dirty khaki pants and red bandanas on their foreheads. They were shirtless and adorned with what appeared to be small African artifacts. Later I found out that it was believed that the artifacts would provide protection and invincibility in battle. Recognizing that we were civilians and of no threat to them, they told us to move quickly behind their lines with our hands up.

There was broken glass and bullet shells everywhere. It was at that moment that I realized that I was barefoot. I was not the only one. The hot pavement and shells singed my feet as I maneuvered down the highway trying to avoid the debris. About half a mile later, we encountered about fifty more rebel soldiers dressed in khaki uniforms. We slowed down with our hands up over our heads and followed their instructions. The rebels directed us into a compound surrounded by a high fence. A lot of people from the neighborhood were there and one by one we reunited with all of our family members who had scattered out of the house that morning.

As we waited in the courtyard, the rebels separated men and women into opposite sides of the compound. Beindu screamed as pa handed her to one of our female cousins. I could see the reluctance and fear in his eyes but there was nothing that he could do. There were a lot of people screaming and clinging onto one another. No one knew what would happen next. I felt like this was it. I'm too young to die. Just that morning, I enjoyed innocent play with my brothers and now my life would end at the tender age of eleven.

Within a few minutes, a young rebel soldier approached pa and said, "What ya tribe?"

Pa replied, "I am Mende."

Obviously not believing that pa was from the Mende tribe, the soldier got more serious. "I will ask you one more time. What ya tribe?"

Pa again responded, "I'm a Mende from Grand Cape Mount County."

The rebel said, "You look like Mandingo."

I'm not sure how it all started but apparently there was some strife between the rebels and the Mandingo tribe. The Mandingo men often had large beards. As a Muslim, pa also wore a large beard so he fit the profile. The rebel asked him to speak Mende. Pa answered in Mende saying hello. I was so afraid for him and wanted them to leave him alone. I was relieved when others from the neighborhood vouched for him. We had lived amongst and befriended several of the families for nearly five years so they were familiar with our background. Even with that being said, it would be one of many times that pa would have to defend his tribal heritage.

The rebels said that we were at the frontline and fighting would continue to escalate between them and the government troops. They told us to continue traveling behind their lines into the territory that had already been captured. They valiantly proclaimed that they were freedom fighters delivering us from the hands of an oppressive government. They seemed confident in telling us that we would be able to return home within seventy-two hours. I didn't know what to believe. It was all so contradictory. They came to my neighborhood, shot through my house and harassed my pa. Not to mention, I had not seen a single government troop in sight that day. How then, could they say that they were coming to free me? Free me from what? I looked to the adults for confirmation but all I saw was fear. The rebels released the women to rejoin us and the walk through hell began.

2 APOCALYPSE

The rebels were like a pack of vicious wolves thirsting to rip apart our flesh.

Our family was amongst a group that had grown to one thousand or more with people steadily coming. As we walked, the sky immediately opened up. It was surreal as if nature sensed our sorrow and could not help but to weep with us. Everything that we had ever known would be no more. We were headed into uncertainty with only the clothes on our backs and memories of yesterday. In the midst of the silence, I thought about ma. *Where was she and how was she? Was she even alive?*

By midday, the sun began to peak out. We saw what appeared to be a water stand. Not knowing when the next drink would be available, a few of us ran up to grab water. Suddenly, a soldier drew his weapon and yelled, "Get da fuck in line!" We quickly obliged. As we continued walking, it was obvious that we were headed deeper into rebel territory. They were everywhere, walking up and down the highway with their assault rifles and standing about menacingly. Unlike those that we encountered at the compound, these soldiers seemed amateur. Some were dressed like civilians, while others stood completely naked or wore outlandish outfits. I wondered why grown men would wear diapers, wedding dresses, lingerie, colorful wigs...you name it. It was bizarre and very creepy. They watched our every move and screamed threats as we passed.

"I will kill you!"

"I will fuck ya ma pussy!"

The rebels were like a pack of vicious wolves thirsting to rip apart our flesh. I just looked down and kept moving. There was checkpoint after checkpoint where we were ushered into a single file line. Each encounter grew increasingly hostile. They questioned who we were, where we came from and what tribe we belonged to. If a person looked like they belonged to an opposing tribe, they were yanked from the line and killed. Their lifeless bodies were kicked down into the ditch alongside the road. People were overtaken with fear not wanting to bring attention to themselves or their family. It turned into a sick, twisted game with some rebels taunting that they had not killed anyone in a while. They would then randomly grab people, who begged for their lives, and shoot them without hesitation. All humanity was lost.

Body parts were cut from the dead and worn around the rebel's necks like medallions. Decomposed human heads sat about on tables and were affixed to the front of vehicles as hood ornaments. It was as if hell itself had taken human form and come up from the abyss. I was petrified! My limbs shook uncontrollably and no matter what I did to mask it, I could not. My mind said, do something, but my fight-or-flight urge was paralyzed by fear. I mean, I had seen my brothers slaughter chickens before and could barely stand to watch it, but this was a whole other level. To witness life being drained from a human being was unimaginable. It ripped away part of my inner most being.

We continued walking down the Monrovia-Kakata Highway as part of a massive group. Like migrant birds, we flocked together hoping to avoid the hawks that lurked nearby. If only we were so lucky. A young man in his teens stopped us. I will never forget him because oddly enough he was wearing a business suit and dress shoes with an assault rifle on his back.

"You! Come here!" he said, pointing at pa.

Pa stepped out of the line, keeping Beindu and I very close to his side.

"What ya tribe?"

"I am Mende."

"Speak it."

"*Mendemo ange,*" pa confidently repeated what he had just said but this time in Mende.

The man snickered. "You learn dat somewhere? Trying to fool me?"

"No," pa replied.

While they were talking, there was movement in the grass next to them. Somehow I did not notice him before, but there laid a man amongst the brush just a few feet away. He wore a white t-shirt and grey slacks. I imagined that he too had been pulled from the line not too long ago. He faced the opposite direction exposing a wound to his neck. Bright red blood stained the top part of his shirt. Taking his attention away from pa, the well-dressed man called for his comrade to come over.

"Ay, my man. I don't tink da man die yet-oh!" He jokingly pointed at the man on the ground who his partner obviously had failed to finish off. Without hesitation, a single shot rang out. It was so loud that I nearly jumped out of my skin. I turned my head. I could not bear the sight. *Oh my God, would this also be my pa's fate!*

"Get back in line." I breathed a sigh of relief. By midafternoon, the rain fell again giving my bare feet a little relief from the hot pavement. We approached a curb and were bombarded by a stench unlike anything that I had ever smelled before. It wreaked of decay and rotten flesh, all confined to an incubator and unleashed at that very moment. I covered my nose but the smell was overpowering. I gagged, as did many others, wondering where it was coming from. The handful of rebel soldiers stationed about, seemed unmoved by the awful odor. As we rounded the curb, there sat a few houses alongside the road. They had all been charred by fire. Their roofs were collapsed and black soot stained the walls that still remained. Perhaps its former occupants had been forced to flee, or God forbid, fell victim to heavy artillery. I could not help but to think about my own home and whether or not it still stood. As we passed by, I could see into the back yard and there lay the source of the foul odor. A mound of twenty or so dead bodies piled on top of one another like a heap of garbage prepared for burning. I spoke not a word. I wondered what type of savages could take innocent lives, obviously without remorse, and return to face such a horrific deed. It was a complete absence of humanity or perhaps an absence of consequences.

A little way down the road, there was a small bridge with a river running under it. We noticed some people drinking so my family decided to stop and rest. I was exhausted emotionally and physically. Pa said since the embankment was not that big that our family should take turns going down. Beindu and I joined him first as the others waited on top of the bridge. Pa told us to use our hands to scoop the water. As we were drinking, I noticed an object floating in the water some fifteen feet away. I continued slurping from my hands as the object approached. By now, others noticed it too. It was a swollen dead body of what appeared to be a middle-aged man clothed in blue jeans and a yellow t-shirt. As he floated by on his back, his shirt rose up over his protruding abdomen which looked like it was about to burst. His skin peeled in some areas exposing the flesh beneath. I slowed my scooping watching the river carry him peacefully to wherever. Ironically, no one stopped drinking or spoke of what we had just witnessed. We just finished and headed back to the main road.

As the rain slowed, the full sun emerged and the asphalt began to heat up once more. By now, my feet had blistered and I could feel them throbbing. Nevertheless, I did not complain because we had to keep going. We walked for about five more miles and came to a place where there was half-eaten cassava all over the road. Cassava is similar to a yucca or potato. Everyone ran and fought over the scraps. Pa managed to get a few and gave it to us. Having seen the bite marks on it, I refused to eat it.

He looked me directly in the eyes and said, "If you do not eat, you will die!" I believed his words and ate all that I was given. It did not taste good raw but it was something to keep me going.

By 7:00 p.m. the sun was setting and the rain came down. We came to an abandoned factory surrounded by a rubber plantation. The front of the factory was fenced and manned by rebel soldiers. We passed easily and joined the crowd of thousands already there. The building itself was two story, gray in color and appeared to be made of tin and concrete. Stairs led up to its roof. Nearby, there was a standing water tower. Machinery and rubber blocks also laid about on the ground. Clothing drenched, we made our way through the people and the thick muddy grounds.

When we finally got inside the factory, the atmosphere was overwhelmed with agony. Amongst the flickering of lanterns, I could see people all throughout the building. Young, old…it did not matter, the flashing faces all showed sorrow and despair. I wondered if some of them had witnessed their loved ones being killed or perhaps been made orphans that very day. I realized that war does not discriminate. It rips through like a tornado, destroying everything in its path and just like that moves on without looking back. As we moved about, I could see people sitting huddled together while others slept. Our group separated finding space wherever it was available. Pa, Beindu, Boakai, Curtis and myself found an open spot with piles of plastic and decided to lay there. As we settled in, there was very little talking. The silence amplified the whimpering, which echoed from every direction. I laid there staring blankly into the darkness. We were near a huge tin loading door so all night I could hear the rain trying to force its way in. Finally, it succeeded in seeping under the door creating puddles on the plastic. With no way of drying or covering ourselves, it was chilly and miserable. Needless to say, there was not much sleeping that night. I spent most of the time thinking about ma and if we would ever see her again. I replayed all that had transpired that day. It was like a living nightmare that I could not awaken from.

The next morning there was mud everywhere so I tied plastic bags around my feet. Since it was the rainy season, I was accustomed to the conditions. As we exited the building, people quietly gathered around fires, so we joined them. Our other relatives came out shortly thereafter. In the midst of the silence, my stomach growled and I wondered where our next meal would come from. Just then, my thought was abruptly interrupted by the yelling of rebel soldiers who stormed the area in a green Toyota pickup truck. They jumped out cursing, brandishing weapons and demanding that we leave the compound. I guess the response was too slow because the next thing I knew, gunfire rang out and melee ensued. People screamed with panic trying to get out of harm's way. The unlucky ones were struck to the ground with clubs and machetes.

My family and I took off running towards the Monrovia-Kakata Highway where once again we were ushered into a single file line. As we neared the checkpoint, there was a group of about fifty rebel soldiers interrogating people and checking their belongings. I walked with my head down in hopes that no one would bother me.

"Hey you!" a voice yelled not too far from where we stood. I kept looking down. "You fucka YOU!" the voice screamed with agitation.

I looked up and saw a soldier, wearing a dingy lab coat and a bright red wig, quickly approaching my oldest brother Opa. By the time he raised his hand to gesture whether or not the soldier was talking to him, he was thrown to the ground.

"Boss man. B-b-boss man," he stuttered, as he lifted his body to a sitting position with his hands up in surrender. He was obviously afraid.

"Shut up and get da fuck on da ground!"

Opa immediately laid back on the pavement placing his hands by his side like a stiff corpse. No one said anything or moreover did anything. We all watched helplessly as the rebel got down on one knee and yanked Opa's head back exposing his throat. When he reached into his jacket pocket and whipped out a kitchen knife, my heart sank. Time slowed and all I could hear was my brother's heartbeat. It was rhythmic...*boom-boom*...*boom-boom*. His eyes squeezed shut and he gritted his teeth. His leg shook profusely. The callous barbarian had the most sinister look on his face as he slid the blade across Opa's throat. I watched the blood trickle down his neck and I thought that he was dead. Inside, I screamed for help but the words knew better than to escape my lips. I felt guilty that the thought of not wanting anyone to know that he was my brother was at the forefront of my mind.

The soldier stood up chuckling. He nudged Opa with his foot and said, "Get up man! I jus' messing wit' you!"

Opa opened his eyes and rose slowly holding his throat. He walked back over to the line and one of our cousins discreetly handed him a scarf from her head, which he tied around his neck. We continued moving in silence. Just ahead, another man was drug by his arms from the line. He screamed for mercy as a group of five rebels bashed his face with sticks and stomped on his flailing body. As soon as he managed to break free, he was shot. The line kept moving. My legs felt lifeless as if I were floating. All emotions escaped me and life hung in the balance. We were all pawns easily discarded at the whims of monsters, some of whom were younger than me. The line slowed down. Ahead was a checkpoint where everyone was being interrogated about their tribal descent. As we waited, a soldier approached us. He looked like he was barely twenty years old, yet an experienced killer. His eyes were red and both his clothing and hands were stained with blood.

He stared at pa and in a very loud voice said, "You! Get over here!"

Pa pulled my sister and me close to him and we stepped out of the line. I thought, *here we go again*, as the soldier asked about pa's tribe. He calmly replied that he was a Mende.

"You tink I stupid, huh?"

"No, I tell you the trut'! I'm a –"

"You a damn liar! You a dirty Mandingo!"

Pa raised his hands in submission. "Please, let me show you." He reached into his pocket handing the man his work identification. "I am what I say. Check my identification. I work for VOA."

The soldier knocked the card out of pa's hand and raised his AK-47. "SHUT UP! I WILL KILL YOU TODAY!" His words pierced my soul and I knew that this was it.

"Please!" pa begged. His plea fell on deaf ears. The soldier used his rifle to shove him to the edge of the road.

Beindu and I clung helplessly to his side. "No, please!" Pa clasped his hands together praying for mercy. "Deez are my chil'ren. Dey will not survive!"

With a quick snap, the soldier cocked his rifle and at point blank range pulled the trigger.

"Pa-paaaaaa!" Beindu screamed. I cringed but the gun never went off!

Pa was still standing! His desperation intensified. "PLEASE, DON'T DO DIS. MY CHIL'REN, PLEASE!"

Meanwhile, the soldier took out the clip and attempted to dislodge the bullet. It took him several tries before he was able to cock the gun again. He pointed the barrel at pa's head and pa immediately let go of our hands. My heart dropped knowing that he had accepted his fate.

"Pa-pa, noooooo!" Beindu yanked his arm. I tried the best that I could to pull her away but she was clawing and crying hysterically. I felt powerless. What could I do but recognize the fact that this was the end for my father. If his death was a result of tribal cleansing, then surely my sister and I would be next.

Out of nowhere, another rebel stepped in the middle of them and said, "Da man say he not Mandingo." The two men tussled a bit and pa's would-be killer was overpowered.

In a fit of rage, he yelled, "You tink you free! I will see you! I will kill you!" He continued yelling and cursing as we got back in line.

After making it through the checkpoint, I glanced back and saw him jumping into the back of a pickup truck. I was so relieved and thankful that pa was alive. However, I could not help but think that as long as pa looked the way he did, his troubles would never be over. If we did not find safety soon, someone would succeed in killing him.

The same day, we continued walking along the Monrovia-Kakata Highway for a few hours into mid-afternoon. Eventually, we reached Careysburg. We turned off onto a side road and could finally see our destination. A few of the neighbors followed us after pa explained that we were at his workplace, the satellite relay station for Voice of America (VOA). Pa worked there for over ten years and made pretty good money by Liberian standards. Because the company was owned by the American government, he believed that the rebels would not be able to gain access into the compound. Nevertheless, as we walked towards the gate, we saw rebels coming towards us. They were singing a song in their native language and doing a celebratory dance around a man that they had with them. He had been stripped of his clothing and his hands were tied behind his back. The man had bruises all over his body and cuts on his face. They took pleasure in beating their captive as he cried and begged for his life. Some menacingly scraped their machetes on the road creating sparks near his feet. As they neared us, they turned up their theatrics, singing even louder and taunting us with their blades. We quickly dropped our heads in submission, but honestly, we were of no concern to them. They had another objective in mind. They forged by us laughing and maintaining their jovial demeanor about their sacrificial offering. The man was led into the sugar cane field that lined the side of the road. A few minutes later, we heard a single gunshot. When we turned to look, we could see machetes going up and down. I asked myself who could butcher a lifeless man into pieces. To see my people taking life with such ease sickened me. We had become a nation of killers of our own brothers. I no longer wanted to be a Liberian. Just then, I felt pa's hand on my shoulder nudging me to hurry along towards the VOA facility. We were met by a rebel checkpoint just ten feet from the gate.

"Single file, single file, single file!" they ordered, yelling obscenities as we hurried to form a line. Only a handful of other people filed in behind us.

Just off to our right, a few small houses lined the road.

They appeared to serve as a station for this particular sect of about twenty-five rebels. Suddenly, a door flew open. A naked man stumbled out as if he had been pushed from behind. Quickly in tow were two rebel soldiers. One gripped his gun on each end and used it to shove the man across our path to the other side of the road. The man struggled to maintain his balance. The other soldier walked casually behind them with a rifle slung over his back.

"I beg you-oooooooohhh! Please don't kill me!" the man pled over and over again. They spoke not a word.

I felt mortified and frightened for the poor man who stood wearing only a pair of black hiking boots. As if killing him was not enough, they stripped him of all dignity. The soldier quickly swung his rifle toward the man and shot him in the chest with three quick bursts. The blast caused him to stagger backwards.

Now in a hovered position, another soldier yelled, "He got *zigeh*," an artifact commonly believed to give its wearer invincibility. "Shoot da fucker in da head man!"

Just like that, the first soldier obliged and the man's brains splattered everywhere as his body dropped into a puddle. It was the most horrific thing that I had ever witnessed. I fought back tears trying not to bring any attention to myself. The line was silent as we cleared the checkpoint.

3 MIRAGE

No one would ever mess with us on American soil.

We reached the Voice of America (VOA) gate which had fencing on each side topped with barbed wire. We were questioned by the company's uniformed security guards. Pa showed his work identification and they explained that since he was an employee that we would be granted housing. As we cleared the gate, I was now able to see the surroundings. It was like a page out of a magazine that somehow was displaced. The grounds were absolutely beautiful and appeared to be professionally landscaped. I had never seen grass so green and edged to perfection. Large palms were scattered about and a lush golf course set off in the distance amongst the rolling hills. It was a haven in the midst of mayhem and I finally felt safe.

Within a few minutes, security escorted us to a housing area. They said it had been vacated by American workers and their families once the war began. There was a mix of one and two story white apartment buildings with open-air walkways and private entrances. Black metal guardrails lined the stairways leading up to the second floor units. Everything was so neat and clean.

Once we got into a downstairs apartment, there were about fifty people inside the main living area. Some rested while others watched television. At first glance, I could see that the unit was very modernized in comparison to my house. It had carpet throughout and I was excited to see what appeared to be an American television station. Led by security, we carefully maneuvered through the cramped space stepping over people before reaching a bedroom. Once unlocked, security said that we could have the room, which included two twin beds and a small nightstand. By now our group had grown to twenty-nine people including our neighbors. Realizing that it was impossible to fit everyone into a space of about twelve by twelve feet, it was decided that the women and children would get the bedroom while the rest of us slept in the main living area.

Pa reported to work immediately leaving us with the other adults. I'm not sure as to what his sense of urgency was, but I hoped that his dedication improved our chances of staying at VOA until the war was over. Our new housemates gave us greens and a few cups of rice. The women in our group used it to prepare a meal for us. There was hardly enough for everyone so one bowl was prepared for all of the boys. Somehow I missed the call because by the time I got there, most of the food was gone. I physically fought over what was left and ended up with two handfuls. This would be the second night that I would go to bed hungry.

Since food was hard to come by, a few of us boys scavenged the nearby forest. We found bananas, oranges, papaya and sugarcane, which we shared with our group. We spent a lot of time exploring the grounds and found out that VOA had its own airstrip, water treatment system and power plant. One day, Opa, Opi and I were walking and noticed that the fence line stopped. While it appeared from the front entrance that the entire facility was enclosed, it was all an illusion. I asked my brothers if they were scared that the rebels would be able to sneak in and they said no. They emphasized that no one would ever mess with us on American soil.

Not too far from our apartment was a tall Acacia mangium tree. It became my favorite place to go alone to sit and think. This was something that I liked to do back home, so in a way it gave me solace. My thoughts were mostly about ma, hoping that she was still alive and wishing to hear her voice just one more time.

"BK-lowwwwww!" she would say. That was her nickname for me that dated back to my birth. To her, *Brima Kemokai Low* had a ring to it. I have to admit, it sounded really good in song. Her return from work was often the highlight of my day. A lot of times, she brought home food from her patients who otherwise would not have been able to pay for her nursing services. I would anxiously await her arrival by standing at the end of the road leading up to our house. My goal was to get her treats early before any of my siblings had a chance to get in on the action. I had gotten so bad that eventually she gave me yet another nickname, *The Gobbler!* I wore the name proudly.

About a week after arriving, I was sitting under the tree and noticed a petite woman dressed in a white nurse's uniform coming up the road. I stared intensely and thought that she looked like ma but I was not sure. I got up and slowly walked toward her to get a closer look. When I realized it was ma, I took off running and leapt into her arms. She cried with great joy and held me ever so closely. Time seemed to slow down. Tears streamed down my face as I replayed her words of caution for us not to go to school

23

on the morning of July 2. *Why would she go to work that day?* She always put our family before herself. As I leaned back in her arms, I could see that she had been through hell to find us. Her hair, normally in place, was disheveled under her nurse's hat. Her uniform, typically pressed to perfection, was stained throughout. She gazed at me with her brown eyes trying to speak but the words would not come out. She did not have to say anything because her eyes said it all.

"Where Lamin? Where everybody?" she asked, putting me back down. She always called pa by his last name.

"He at work. Everybody inside."

She followed me to the apartment and reunited with the rest of the group. They were all overjoyed to see her! "MMP on the Attack!" they joked, calling her by her alter ego. You see, ma had a long-standing reputation for being a spitfire! She was one of the nicest people that you would ever meet, but if you crossed her...watch out! So the adults were not surprised that MMP, short for "Marie Maima Perry", her maiden name, had no problems making it through the war zone!

That night, the group gathered around an open fire. The women cooked the few pounds of cow meat that ma brought with her. She explained that the rebel soldiers had given it to her for delivering sixty babies over the prior three days. I was so amazed that ma accomplished such a feat and that the rebels openly rewarded her for it. Everyone shared war stories with each account as horrific as the next. Some talked about witnessing decapitations while others saw babies being carved out of their mother's wombs. Rapes were far too common and the mere mention of the word "*tybay*" sent shivers down my spine. Such a method of torture, in which the elbows of the victim were pulled together at the back and tied with wire, was unimaginable. To make matters worse, a straight edge razor was used to rip through the chest cavity. I was shocked to hear that some of the heinous acts were committed by the government troops. Here I thought they were protectors of the people.

Ma sat there quietly and I wondered if her silence was any indication that she too had been victimized at the hands of soldiers. I was not sure if I wanted to know the truth. Eventually she opened up and shared that a few hours after arriving to work that morning, she heard over the radio that the rebels had attacked our neighborhood. She begged one of the doctors to drive her home. He was only willing to drop her off to his neighborhood, ELWA Junction in Paynesville, some five miles from our house. She walked to a relative's house nearby and surprisingly they were home. They all remained inside and locked down throughout the night as gunfire rang out. The next morning, despite warnings not to go, ma decided to walk on the backroads determined to reach home. The streets were unusually empty. Once she reached the Red Light District, she could not believe what she saw. This normally bustling marketplace was completely ravished with dead bodies and bullet shells all over the streets. In the midst of the still, a young girl came darting from behind a house. Ma heard the voice of a man scream "Stop!" Not having seen him, she did not know whether he was talking to her or the girl. Ma stopped immediately and raised her hands in the air but the girl kept running. A single shot rang out and the girl's body fell to the ground. The rebel soldier walked towards ma and asked where she was going. She responded and he told her to hurry along. Ma turned away, trying to quickly step over the bodies. Laughing, the rebel told her to go ahead and step on them.

She finally reached our house and was met by nearly a dozen rebels. Some were out front slaughtering and cooking our chickens, while others casually walked in and out of the front door. One rebel questioned why she was there and held her at gunpoint. Just then, one of our neighbors came out of our house. He told the soldiers not to kill her. She could not believe what she was witnessing. This neighbor, who was of Gio descent, had joined the rebels. He asked her if she wanted to come inside and gather some belongings but she declined. He advised that more than likely, we were at the Omega Tower facility so he walked her there.

At Omega, ma navigated her way through the crowd, which she estimated, had grown to over a thousand people. No one had seen us. Still wearing her nurse's uniform, almost immediately she was grabbed by civilians and rebels alike to assist with delivering babies. Because of the stress of the war, many women went into premature labor. According to ma, there were many other medical staff there from the hospital that she worked at, but they hid themselves. Some thought that if they came forward, they might be perceived as "government allies" considering that the prominent hospital was government owned. Putting that aside, ma readily helped as needed. As soon as she delivered and wrapped one baby, she had to quickly move on to the next person. With overcrowded conditions and a shortage of food, ma could only hope for the best outcomes for the new mothers and their babies. I was so proud of her and thankful that she was back with us safe and sound at VOA!

By August, the war continued to rage on and thousands came to VOA seeking refuge. The conditions became tough in the *camp* as some people called it. Housing was limited so most laid their heads wherever they could, making shelter from bamboo, palm leaves and other raw materials found in the forest. The grounds quickly changed showing visible signs of increased population. The beautiful golf course was worn from foot traffic and now served as a lot for a community of huts. People relieved themselves wherever they could so sanitation became an issue as well as the smell. Soon the power and water was turned off so we cooked outside and fetched drinking water from a little stream that ran through the property. Resources, especially food, were minimal. Over time, I lost nearly twenty pounds and had to use a rope to hold up my shorts. I decided to try fishing. It was new to me but hunger drove me to do all that I could for food. I thinned out a shoestring and attached it to a stick. I bent a safety pin to form a hook and added it to the end of the string. For bait, I dug up worms in the forest. To my surprise, I caught a catfish on my first fishing attempt. Soon it became a daily routine and I always shared my catch with our group. We ate it, in addition to bush meat and finely chopped, young palm leaves called "palm cabbage". I still walked around barefoot wearing the same yellow t-shirt and brown shorts that I arrived in one month prior. Each day the other boys and I walked about a mile to take a bath and wash our clothes. We stood naked in the bushes while our clothes dried. I was excited when pa brought me a pair of pants, a shirt and tennis shoes that he kept in his locker at work. Even though the clothes were too big, I made them work.

I began to take notice of a girl from my neighborhood named Esther. She was very pretty with big brown eyes and deep set dimples. Her braids flowed down her back only to be outdone by her figure, which was definitely coming into its own. All of the boys vied for her attention and could not understand why she, being sixteen years old, would take interest in an eleven year-old. I was certainly mature for my age, yet and still eleven and she knew it. Despite the ridicule from the kids her age, Esther spent most of her free time with me. Since she was responsible for helping to prepare and serve the food, she often snuck me extra food after the shared mealtime. Eventually, she became my girlfriend.

One night, Esther managed to find a spot near me in the common sleeping area. It was dark so I started touching and fondling her. My heart raced with excitement knowing that I was about to have sex for the first time. All the years of hearing stories from my older brothers and now it would be my turn. I wished I had asked more questions on exactly what to do. I tried to remember the images that I saw in the porno magazines stuffed under Opa's bed or the scenes from the video that my friend's pa brought back from America. I could not seem to gather my thoughts. Esther tried pulling me on top of her but I was too afraid of getting caught. Although the "birds and bees" conversation was never had with me, I knew that sex was something that only adults should do. Luckily for me, Esther took the lead. The next thing I knew, we were having sex. Within a few minutes my body trembled uncontrollably and just like that, it was over. The next day, I could not wait to tell my friends and of course they asked her. I thought that she would have been angry, but she just smiled and validated my manhood. I was walking high and found myself sleeping next to Esther many nights while at VOA!

There was a small medical clinic already established so ma quickly submerged herself back into her true calling as a head nurse. Armed with nothing more than her bare hands, a towel and a bucket of warm water, once again she became the go-to person for delivering babies. Ma was a master of her craft and the babies were rolling off the assembly line. Her name quickly spread across the camp. Even the dark of the night did not stop her. Often times people knocked at the apartment door asking for ma as their loved ones went into labor. Her pay consisted of words of thanks, or perhaps a cup of rice or cassava. She loved what she did and to me she was a hero who brought life to the camp. Having ma around gave me a sense of normalcy and the security of home.

Pa continued to work most days. Opi, Opa and I visited him every two weeks. The purpose of the mile and a half trek was two-fold...to deliver messages and to transport his laundry back and forth for washing by yours truly. The employee work area was extremely secure. In fact, we had to pass through another manned gate and await phone authorization from pa before we could enter the area. He met us in the lobby wearing his hard hat, khaki pants and boots. His walkie-talkie was strapped to his side and the infamous beard was completely shaved! I was thankful for that. As a special treat, sometimes he took us into the power plant. The gigantic turbines nearly blew my eardrums out.

The workers seemed pretty tight knit. Since they maintained sleeping quarters there, they shared in responsibilities like cooking. Pa's day was Friday, so he usually relinquished the responsibility to us. We prepared rice and soup and always made sure to sit some aside for ourselves. Once in a while, pa gave us MRE's (Meals Ready-to-Eat). He called it military food. We had all kinds of stuff like chicken, barbeque pork, pound cake and crackers. I figured if the American military ate this good, than the citizens must be really well off.

From our trips back and forth visiting pa, I took notice of all the unmanned access points throughout the property with trails leading into the forest. I started to wonder how safe we really were. Not only were rebel forces stationed just outside of the gate but they could easily come in from other areas and who would stop them. VOA no longer felt like a sanctuary but rather a mirage and we were desert wanderers.

By September, people grew comfortable with the surroundings and went outside the gates to buy food and goods from locals and even the rebels. No one seemed to care that the items were most likely stolen or previously owned by someone who was now deceased. The general belief was that we were just waiting for the war to end. Then late one afternoon, truckloads of armed rebel soldiers stormed the compound. I was surprised to see them inside the property and knew that something must have gone horribly wrong. *Where were the security guards who manned the gates? Why would the rebels dare enter the American owned property?*

The rebels demanded that we quickly grab our belongings and leave. People scattered, gathering what they could and ran towards the exit. Those who moved slowly were beaten and cursed at. I sprinted into the bedroom, grabbed a white sheet and stuffed it with a few items of clothing for myself and pa. My other relatives did the same. As we headed out, we saw the rebels looting and loading up items of value from the different apartments. Here we were, once again leaving our little piece of comfort. Only God knew what was waiting for us outside of those gates. I wondered if pa knew what was going on. Just then, a van approached. As it passed, I could see that it was filled with VOA employees.

"Dere da pa-paye!" I screamed, pointing at the van. "Paaaaaaaaaa!" He couldn't hear me. He was facing forward and with all of the people heading out of the compound, there was no way that he saw us.

"Dey locking him up?" Opi asked, noting that there were rebel vehicles both in front and behind the van. We did not know what was happening. All that we could do in that moment was hope that no harm would come his way and forge ahead.

4 JOURNEY

I had almost forgotten about the nine miles that I walked in my flip flops...but my feet quickly reminded me.

Kakata, the next city along the highway and the capital of Margibi county, was eighteen miles away. We decided to head there carrying what few belongings we managed to grab on top of our heads. Of all things, ma decided to bring a mortar and pestle, used for grinding ingredients. It was so like her to think about feeding the group but utterly ridiculous to believe that she could balance twenty-five pounds of solid wood throughout the duration of our journey. It was a valiant effort but she ditched her prize possession not too long after we set out.

I mostly walked with my brothers and my male cousins. At one point, the conversation came up about whether or not we would ever consider joining the rebels. I knew with absolute certainty that if I had a choice, I would not. My brother Opa and some of my cousins, on the other hand, had a different stance. They talked about the potential for increased hardship on the road ahead. Perhaps, "joining up" would provide a means of survival. I understood where they were coming from, and while a part of me hoped that it would never come to that, another part felt like I too would be protected.

As we continued to walk, we hit several checkpoints. Each time we stopped our belongings were searched. At one checkpoint, we were ushered into a single file line. I was ahead of my family when a soldier pulled out a pair of trousers from my bundle.

"Who dey trouser for?" he asked, holding them up to himself.

"Dey my pa trouser."

"Where he at?"

I paused for a brief second. "He behind me. He coming." I looked down because there was no way I was going to explain that pa got arrested. Before I could raise my head back up, his open hand struck the side of my temple and I lost my footing.

"You lying dummy! Take ya tings and go!"

My head pulsated with pain and I felt woozy. Tears swelled up in my eyes, but I did not let out a sound. I just gathered my things off the ground and watched as he walked away with pa's pants in hand. My family caught up to me at the next checkpoint and I made sure that I stayed with them from that point on.

We walked most of the day along the Monrovia-Kakata Highway. People started to spread out and soon we were down to our group of twenty-nine including the neighbors. Just as night was about to fall, we stumbled upon a small village of six mud huts located along the stretch of highway. It was stationed by a rebel soldier holding a .22 caliber long rifle by his side. As we approached, he seemed at ease slowly walking our way. He appeared to be in his early twenties yet aged by whatever struggles life had thrown his way. His civilian clothes were filthy and as he opened his mouth to speak, he was missing several of his front teeth.

"Wha' you won?" he asked, trying to find out what we wanted. The adults explained that we were told to leave VOA and now headed to Kakata. They asked if we could stop there for the night. The soldier agreed. As we waited, he walked over and spoke with a few villagers. Within ten minutes, an older woman carrying a lantern motioned for us to follow her. She smiled as she led us to a hut instructing us to leave our belongings outside. Inside, there were hay bales aligning the circular wall for seating and lying down. With the exception of a large kerosene lantern, the middle of the hut was completely open so we grabbed some blankets from our things and spread them across the dirt floor. We knew that it would be tight but at this point we had grown accustomed to making any space work. Not soon after, the woman invited us to grab a bite to eat.

We followed her to the outside kitchen some forty yards away. As we approached the pavilion log structure, we could see a wood-burning fire in the center with smoke escaping through the hole strategically placed in the palm leaf roof. It seemed as though this was not a regular meal time because most of the people went about their normal routine and only two women and the soldier joined us. We were given three large metal bowls with rice and palm oil and three additional bowls filled with water.

Ever since the war started, we had gotten used to splitting up into our shared meal groups consisting of females & toddlers, male children and male young adults. This time was no exception. I was in the male children's group. We washed our hands with some of the water and then formed a circle on the ground with our two bowls in the middle. My cousin James, the oldest in our group, stuck his finger in the rice and stirred it about quickly to mix in the palm oil. From the look on his face, the food just came off of the fire. At random or perhaps out of greed, my brother Curtis started the food rotation. He used the side of the bowl to scoop a level size amount of rice into his hand. Ma called me "The Gobbler", but honestly he had me beat by a long shot. Back home, he would ask for everyone's bowls after dinner and lick them. He would gather leftover bones and suck the marrow out before chewing them like it was nothing. Boy was he greedy! After Curtis took his turn, the process continued clockwise until everyone had their turn. With each round, everyone took care to change their portion size so that each person got their equal share. We were on our best behavior that night but at VOA we had several fights over food. Curtis was the biggest culprit of overfilling his hand with mounds of whatever was being served. We called him out on it, but he was so greedy that sometimes he quickly shoved the food into his mouth pretending not to understand what all of the fuss was about.

In general, war changed people's attitudes about food and water. I understood it in the sense of limited supply and growing demand but sometimes things seemed to be over the top. There was this unspoken process and etiquette surrounding shared eating. If you stepped outside of the boundaries, you were quickly roped back in by choice or force. I thought that I had committed a crime at VOA when I decided that rather than eating immediately during the food rotation, I would place each one of my scoops into my own personal bowl to be consumed afterwards. Some kids called me a cheater, while others said that I thought that I was better than them. Really, all I wanted to do was eat my food in private and at my own pace. What was the harm in that? Well, the other kids certainly took offense. They complained so much that one of the adults living in the apartment asked me never to do that again.

As we sat there eating in the village, I could not help but notice the soldier checking out my girlfriend.

"Wha' you name?" he asked, looking directly at her.

"Esther," she replied, quickly turning back to her food.

He walked over to Opa, kneeled down and placed his hand on his shoulder as if they were friends and asked, "My man...her got husmon?"

I was so angry. What would make him think that Esther would ever be interested in him? He was country and could barely speak English. I mean, we all spoke broken English, even I knew that from watching British programming, but he was horrible. The villagers seemed so comfortable with him that I could only assume that he was originally from there. Perhaps a wannabe or maybe an actual recruit left behind to cover an area so far behind rebel lines that the likelihood of him having to engage in combat was slim. He was a nobody. Yet and still, he held the gun and therefore all of the power.

Having overheard the soldier's question to my brother, Esther glanced over at me. Apparently, my look clearly communicated what her response should be. "No" she spoke up, trying to take the pressure off my brother.

The soldier smirked exposing his snaggletooth as he walked over taking a seat on a log near the women's group. He went on complimenting Esther about her looks. It was very uncomfortable because he seemed so desperate. I wondered if there were any other young women in the village. All I seen up until that point were older people. What if he forced himself on Esther? What could I do? I felt so sorry for her. I could tell that she was nervous and probably having similar thoughts. Nonetheless, she remained polite and took care not to upset him. Before we headed back to the hut to turn in for the night, he approached the women and told them that he wanted Esther to remain there in the village with him. He promised to protect her. The women thanked him for his offer and explained that we were a family and could not be separated. Luckily, he accepted.

The next morning, we woke and ate cassava with palm oil before heading back out. I had almost forgotten about the nine miles that I walked in my flip flops the day before, but my feet quickly reminded me. They throbbed, as did my back, from carrying the large bundle of clothes on top of my head. We were still only halfway to Kakata. By the time we reached the rebel checkpoint, the bundle loosened and covered my eyes so that I did not notice the rebel soldier staring at me.

He walked over and knocked it off my head to get my attention. "Why you hiding?" he yelled.

I froze. "I–I not hiding." I tried to muster up my nerve. "My bundle loosen. I swear, I not hiding."

"Liar!" he snapped, with his finger in my face. "You enemy! Open it!" he ordered.

As I bent over, he pushed me to the side and snatched my bundle open. I looked around for ma but she and the others were also being interrogated. I hoped that this would pass quickly. Surely, he would not find anything of concern. He rummaged through the clothing and lifted up a few of pa's shirts.

Realizing that they were too big for me he said, "You steal it?"

I thought, *here we go again, another rebel asking questions about pa's clothing.* If only the VOA raid had not taken place during the same week that I had pa's laundry or perhaps if I owned more than three outfits, I would have packed my bundle with my own stuff.

"I ain't steal it. Dey my pa."

"Where he at?"

"I don't know." I figured that I'd answer honestly, giving him only what he needed to know.

"What you mean you not know where your pa is?"

"I just don't know." I could not understand why he was

so angry. Was this just a show to steal my things? His torn t-shirt and faded black pants certainly looked like they had seen better days but why the need for the dramatics. I mean, he stood there with an AK-47 in his hand, for God's sake. Perhaps he was embarrassed that as a grown man he was reduced to stealing from an eleven-year old.

Before I knew it, he yanked his black leather belt from his belt loops and struck me repeatedly on my back. Each lash stung my skin and the tears quickly streamed down my face. The soldier picked up the clothing that he wanted from the ground and walked away. I guess my suspicions about his motives were right. I gathered the remaining items, tossed them into my dirty sheet and tied it back into a bundle. As I lifted the sack to my head, I made eye contact with ma. She looked so helpless. I turned and walked away and the group followed suit without speaking a word.

By early evening, we finally reached Kakata. We were met by rebel soldiers who told us that we could not enter the city because night would soon be falling. They said that we could stay nearby at Booker T. Washington Institute. We were amongst a few hundred who slept in classrooms that night.

The next morning our group combined money and some of the adults went into town to buy some food. Upon return, they cooked on an open fire and we ate. By mid-morning, ma and some of the others went to search for relatives who lived in the city. While she was gone, pa came to the school looking for us. We were so excited to see that he was alive! He explained that after he and the other VOA employees were detained, they were transported to Kakata. He had spent the past two days looking for us amongst the new arrivals. He asked where ma was and I told him that she had gone into town.

Ma returned later that day. She too was excited to see pa and to share the news that she had found my grandmother. We would now have a place to stay and the neighbors were invited to come as well. At that time, pa's relatives who had previously come from Grand Bassa County to live with us decided to part ways. My older brothers, Opa and Opi, also decided that they would stay with some friends who lived nearby. I could not believe that they were splitting up the family after all that we had been through. While nine years apart, Opi and I always had a special bond. I admired his "go getter" mentality. In the marketplace, he could negotiate a deal like no other and he always made money. I tagged along behind him hoping that some of what he had would rub off on me. I was too shy though. Somehow I knew that as long as my two brothers stayed together, they would be o.k. That still did not change the fact that I felt abandoned. Hopefully, Kakata would bring about a new start at life for everyone.

5 BORN AGAIN

My faith grew beyond measure and I thirsted for more.

The trip to grandma's place took a few hours by foot. When we arrived, it was just as I remembered it some six years prior. There were two houses sitting on the two-acre lot. They were accented by a backdrop of orange, brown and yellow hues coming from an array of fruit trees scattered throughout the property. The rolling hills stretched out to the edge of the stream. The main house, which had one level, was spacious and beautiful. The guest house was a bit smaller but still offered three bedrooms. A family already occupied one of the bedrooms so our group of eighteen took the remaining two rooms. It was tight, but we managed by sleeping wherever space permitted...hallways, common living areas, you name it.

There was no power in Kakata so we used bottles and rags to make oil lamps. Since kerosene was hard to come by, we improvised by using fuel oil. To stretch our supply, we added water, which caused the oil to float to the top of the bottle. The lamps gave off a lot of smoke, so black soot built up on the ceilings. Each day, we all woke up stuffy so it became a part of the morning routine to remove the black film that had built up in our nostrils overnight.

Kakata was deep behind the rebel lines so there was no fighting and surprisingly the rebels were not hostile. It was very ironic to think that we were now living in a city full of the same people who had just tried to kill us. All we could do was hope for some measure of peace. Within a few days, I parted ways with my first love Esther. Her uncle got word of her whereabouts and came to pick her up. It was bittersweet seeing the joy between the two of them as they reunited, all the while feeling like I may never see her again. As the adults talked inside, we stole away for one last kiss. Butterflies filled my stomach all over again as I thought about the time that we shared. I loved Esther and I needed to let her know. As the words released from my lips, her eyes swelled with tears. She stared at me for a while with her radiant smile before telling me that she loved me too. Her uncle called for her and just like that it was over. I watched them as they disappeared down the trail.

As we settled in Kakata, one of the biggest challenges was having enough food to eat. No one worked so there was no income coming in. Most of the time, we searched the forest for fruits and nuts. There was also a breadnut tree located in between the two houses. It stood over fifty feet tall. While we tried using a slingshot, it was nearly impossible to get to the delectable fruit that hung on the branches. We all had to wait until they dropped. Not only did we wait, but we strategized by taking shifts to ensure that our family members were the first to grab the ripe fruits as they fell to the ground. We were not always successful. Most times, after hearing the thump, we raced to the tree and fought with the other housemates until the fruit broke into pieces. Each fruit yielded about fifty nuts. We boiled them in their shells with salt and then cracked them open to eat. They tasted like potatoes and were very filling. Somehow, outsiders found out about the tree. One morning around 3:00 a.m. I headed outside to pee. I was startled to see a man under the tree looking on the ground for breadnuts. When he saw me, he took off running into the forest.

As a source of income, we cut firewood and sold it to passersby. The profits were used to buy food to eat and the ingredients needed to make food to sell. Kala, a sweet fried bread, was a popular item that ma made in abundance. The other children and I were responsible for walking around the city selling it. We hustled day by day to make ends meets.

One day, a pastor came by to talk to grandma about holding church services on her property. She agreed to allow him to use her yard. While I was curious about the increased traffic to the house, I never took religion seriously. For me, it was more of an obligation involving dictated prayers, trips to the mosque and wearing clothing that made me the subject of a lot of teasing from my friends.

Pa was a devout Muslim who pushed very hard for us to practice the Islamic faith. I certainly lacked the discipline that it took to be a Muslim. With the washing of hands and feet before each of the five daily prayers and the 4:00 a.m. rise time, I found it unbearable. I was especially turned off by the repetitive prayers.

Allahu Akbar. Audhu billahi min ashshayta

Nirrajeem. Bis milla hirrahma nirraheem.

Alhamdu lillahi rabbil aalameen. Arrahmaa

41

nirraheem. Maliki yaumiddeen. Iyyaka nabudu

wa iyyaka nasta'een. Ihdi nassira talmustaqeem.

Sira talladhina anamta alayhim, ghayril maghdubi

alayhim, wa ladhdhaal leen. Aameen.

I never knew what I was saying so there was no personal connection. My focus was on reciting it correctly because I was beaten otherwise.

I was never given a choice on what religion to follow. Pa was raised a Muslim so, according to him, it was the ultimate sin if his children were not Muslims. I had a lot of questions concerning the religion but pa was unwilling to discuss them with me. He once told me with absolute certainty, "Islam is the one true religion that God has chosen and no other religion comes close." I wondered how he knew this to be true. Had he himself spoken to Allah? Curiosity got the best of me so I asked how he knew this to be true. He exploded in anger striking me across my face screaming, "Never ask me that again!"

Out of fear, I followed pa's command but Islam was never in my heart. Neither was Christianity for that matter. I had exposure to it in school because Bible class was a regular part of the curriculum. Pa was certainly aware of this. Not to mention, he met and spent nearly sixteen years with ma who was a Christian. She showed no signs of converting so pa did not want us participating in her religious beliefs or eating habits. Even still, ma would sneak us pig's feet and other pork when he was not home. One day, pa came in from work and discovered ma making soup with pork. He became so angry that he picked up the pot and tossed the whole thing out the front door.

A few weeks after the church was established, I was taking a bath in the outside bathhouse when I overheard people singing "When We All Get to Heaven". Their voices had so much power and I felt drawn to them. I got dressed quickly and rushed over to where they were having service. I felt the power of God moving through the people and in me. There was no real way to explain it other than an overwhelming feeling of joy and sorrow at the same time. I didn't know why I was having all these emotions. It was like I was gaining something and losing something. Tears immediately streamed down my face. My life changed forever. From that moment on, I could not wait for Sundays.

Pa would be indoors thinking that I was outside playing but I was sitting in the far back of the worship service. The pastor taught a lot on hope and faith. He said that despite our circumstances, God was still in control and through faith all things were possible. He taught scriptures from the Bible and the words seemed to jump off the page. It felt so good to know that we would be OK. I believed. My faith grew beyond measure and I thirsted for more. I found myself laying hands on the sick, including myself, and professing healing in the name of Jesus Christ. I was on fire for the Lord and continued to go behind pa's back attending crusades and revivals. While I tried not to draw attention to myself, it was difficult considering that I was the only child amongst all of the adults. Eventually the pastor noticed my regular attendance and pointed it out as a demonstration of faithfulness to the rest of the congregation. He asked me why I liked to come and I explained that I felt the power of God moving in my life simply by believing and trusting Him. Many people could not believe that a young child was speaking this way. The pastor told me that God had a purpose for my life and that He was the one changing me from the inside. It was awesome and spiritually the strongest time of my life.

By Christmas 1990, we had been in Kakata for three months and over five months had passed since we fled from our home. Celebratory gunfire rang out all around the city. We went house to house knocking on doors and rejoicing with our neighbors. Over the next month, we heard rumors that the rebels had been pushed out of the capital city of Monrovia and that the fighting had ceased there. This was a result of the arrival of soldiers called the Economic Community of West African States Monitoring Group (ECOMOG) who represented the Economic Community of West African States (ECOWAS). ECOWAS was an established group of fifteen African nations that worked together.

The news of ECOMOG's arrival, along with the lack of work, prompted pa to try to find a way for us to return home to Paynesville. He explained that there was no direct route because the rebels probably would not allow it. Instead, we would need to travel through several neighboring countries and reenter Liberia in a safe zone. With the plan set, pa left for the Ivory Coast, a country along the eastern border of Liberia. He promised to return for us after he had gathered enough information about the trip. While I was excited about traveling outside of the country for the first time, I was really anxious about returning back home to Paynesville. I didn't know what to expect. From what we heard, the rebels had been pushed out of the capital, but they were very much alive and well in Kakata. As a matter of fact, their numbers continued to grow. Even family and close friends of mine were recruited.

One day, we received a surprise visit from my cousin, James, who parted ways with us at the Booker T. Washington Institute when we first arrived in Kakata. He was with my friends who I had not seen since the day before the war hit my neighborhood. Their chests, arms and wrists were adorned with *zigeh* and I knew immediately that they had joined. Not to mention the fact that James had an AK-74 strapped to his back. I was so happy to see them all. I can't say the same for the adults. They all got quiet and went on about their business. The boys explained that their families were safe. We talked about the good old days and what life was like before the war. I asked a lot of questions about how they joined and they answered that they chose to do so. I tried to avoid the obvious question about whether or not they had killed anyone. Honestly, I was not sure if I wanted to know. I'd much rather remember all of them as they were...my boys from the neighborhood. Then, James dropped a bomb on me.

"BK, you remember Uncle Konah?" Uncle Konah was ma's brother. He visited from time to time, usually when he needed something.

"Yeah, why?"

"He joined. Dey call him Chuck Norris now." I definitely knew who Chuck Norris was. I had become a fan as soon as I saw *Missing in Action* some five years earlier. He was a real badass...sort of like a one-man army.

"Why dey call him Chuck Norris?"

"Da man not scared in fighting-oh! Dey make him Commander quick. He kill plenty people!"

James spoke as if it were no big deal. I thought to myself, *war had a way of bringing out the best and the worst in people.* As he continued talking about how my uncle killed by the dozens at his checkpoint, I could not help but to think about how not too long ago I watched pa being pulled from the line. To know that my own family participated in such heinous acts disgusted me. At the same time, staring into James' eyes, I saw innocence and not that of the bloodshot killers that we encountered along the way. Before I knew it, the visit was over. The three said their goodbyes and headed back down the road.

On January 16, 1991, the British Broadcasting Corporation (BBC) radio station reported that another war was unleashed on foreign soil. The United States and allied forces launched Operation Desert Storm after Iraq failed to withdraw from Kuwait. I wondered why the U.S. would rush to help them but not us. For as long as I could remember, we looked up to America as our big brother. We learned all about how Liberia was founded as a colony for freed American slaves. Eventually, we gained our independence but we still had American influences in our culture and even in our flag. Why would the U.S. abandon us at a time when we needed help the most?

I had a lot of free time on my hands waiting for pa's return, so I got creative and came up with my own theater shows. I loved Jean-Claude Van Damme movies like *Bloodsport* and *Kickboxer* so a lot of my characters were fighters. I made them using cardboard and string. I even created isolation movements in some of the limbs. The backs had strategically placed sticks, enabling me to control them with both my fingers and toes. For a stage, I used a three by five-foot cardboard box and flipped it on its side leaving two openings. One end served as the screen and I covered it with a white sheet. I used the other opening to enter the box. Once inside, I controlled the figures. For lighting, I placed a candle between me and the figures so that only the figure's shadows showed through the curtain. The theater became a favorite evening pastime with everyone gathering in grandma's living room to watch. I even had dialogue and sound effects to go along with the storyline. Curtis served as my assistant and helped with quick scene changes. As word got out, more people attended and we even got donations. It was awesome and I usually ended the night with a standing ovation! I could not believe that I was doing this. I was typically shy in front of large groups but inside the box I could be whomever I wanted to be.

Almost a month had gone by and still no word from pa. Everyone was extremely worried about his well-being. Then one day, a former neighbor drove up asking for ma. He told her that he ran into pa in the Ivory Coast. Due to difficulties experienced on his solo trip, pa would not be returning to accompany us. The neighbor gave ma thirty USD, a few pair of sandals for us boys and a letter explaining our travel arrangements.

When the day arrived for us to leave, it was sad to bid farewell to everyone especially the neighbors who had experienced this journey with us. I felt guilty when ma, my siblings and I headed out to meet the van. Nevertheless, the expedition had to be made.

6 EXPEDITION

I had been in four different countries over a period of just a few days.

Due to unpaved roads and the number of checkpoints, the driver said that the trip to the Ivory Coast would take twice as long. Dust flew everywhere as he maneuvered about in the van trying to avoid potholes. I was relieved that the driver had a rapport with the rebels as he belonged to the same tribe as many of them. It also helped that he gave them money as we passed by. We traveled mostly on the Kakata-Gbarnga Highway, a dirt road that served as a main throughway for both vehicles and foot traffic. As we approached villages, we saw people walking along the road carrying goods on their heads and toting babies on their backs. The driver stopped on a few occasions to rest and we were swarmed by street peddlers selling food and other goods. A common item was cow meat on a stick or at least it was said to be cow meat. Whatever it was, it was dried

48

up and hardly recognizable. It looked like it had been exposed to the sun for days, maybe even weeks. We avoided purchasing food and just waited near the car for the driver.

As we neared Gbarnga, the capital of Bong County, the road became paved and there was a significant amount of rebel presence. The city reminded me of Monrovia in that there was some level of maintenance to the buildings and roads. The driver proudly toted that Gbarnga was home to revered rebel leader, Charles Taylor, and heavily guarded by the rebels or the National Patriotic Front of Liberia (NPFL) as he called them. He was a proud patriot bearing allegiance to the NPFL and their revolution, all fought in the name of freedom. Ironically, he contradicted his depiction of brotherly solidarity each time he lied at a rebel checkpoint about the purpose of our trip. He stuck with the story that we were merchants traveling to the Ivory Coast and we passed without incident.

Shortly after exiting the city, the road returned back to its battered state. Between maneuvering around the massive potholes and pulling over whenever the road narrowed to one passable lane, the 145-mile trip seemed like an eternity. By early evening, we stopped to spend the night at the driver's home in Sanniquellie, the capital of Nimba County. The cottage style house sat on an acre of land surrounded by miniature palm trees. I was pleasantly surprised by the spacious interior complete with exposed wood beam ceilings and a view into the upper level. The driver's family graciously received us as if they were accustomed to overnight guests as a part of his profession. They gave ma rice, meat and oil and she prepared a meal that night. We ate, bathed and quickly turned in for an early start.

The next day we continued our trip toward the Ivory Coast. The border was open and before crossing over, the rebels asked if we intended to come back. The driver said yes and again made up a story about ma being a merchant. By late afternoon, we had covered sixty miles entering the town of Danané, located in the western part of the country near the Guinean and Liberian borders. As we drove into the crowded marketplace, the aroma of roasted lamb and fresh fried kala seeped through the window. I wanted some so bad but had to settle for the fried chicken's feet that ma had tucked away in her bundle from last night's dinner. As I ate, I noticed that most of the people were dressed in traditional Muslim attire. The men sported ankle length robes, while the women wore long dresses and head coverings. There was buying and selling of goods and everything was in motion. The people moved with purpose as if there was no time to waste. I had seen crowded marketplaces before but in this one I felt like an outsider as everyone around conversed in French. Every vehicle seemed specially customized to accommodate more than its intended capacity. Mopeds buzzed by with whole families and vans were chopped to allow for additional cargo such as charcoal or the fresh harvest for sale. Despite the circumstances, I could finally say that I had visited another country.

As we exited the van, pa was waiting for us. We were so happy to see him! He took us back to the place where he was staying and said that we would head out in the morning. It was one of many small, one room efficiency units all connected together in a u-shaped single story building. The aging concrete structure was scarred with chipped yellow paint. Pa had no time to update the décor in his unit, not that he would have anyway, which boasted a few blankets on the floor and a couple of dishes stacked on top of a small wooden end table. His bag of clothing still sat packed in the corner. We all found a place on the floor trying to recuperate from our long journey.

"So pa-pa, how was da road?"

He shook his head and said, "BK, da road was not easy-oh. Dey took most of my money. I was scared to come back."

I felt so bad for pa and was glad that he made it through safely. Curtis, Boakai and I spent the remainder the day sitting in front of the building people watching. We were surprised to see so many Liberians. After making friends with a few other children, we quickly learned that they too were newcomers. Unlike us, most of them seemed like they were settled down with no desire to run back to Liberia.

By the time we woke up, pa had already arranged for a driver to take us into the country of Guinea. Again, he explained that we needed to travel through Guinea in order to reach Sierra Leone. We ate before leaving and ma carried food for us to eat along the way. Including the driver, eight of us packed into the mid-sized sedan. We traveled along dirt roads passing several small villages before reaching the Guinea border around noon. It was protected by French speaking soldiers who allowed us to pass after briefly speaking with the driver. We continued on throughout the day, traveling nearly 150 miles before reaching the town of Macenta located in the southeastern part of the region. It was evening when pa left us waiting at the transportation area while he made arrangements for a taxi to take us to Sierra Leone the following morning. Our next stop was the city of Kenema, which was 160 miles away. It was ideal because both of my parents had family there.

That night we stayed in a rundown motel. It had no electricity or running water and there was a common bathroom shared by the guests. Before turning in for the night, my brothers and I went outdoors to pump bath water. As ma was warming it up on the wood fire, we headed down the road to buy some food.

"So Boakai, you happy you going back to Sierra Leone?"

"Yeah, I happy to go see my people."

"And your girlfriend!" Curtis joked, nudging Boakai with his elbow. "How da place like?"

"It been a long time since I been home-oh." Now fourteen, Boakai came to live with us when he was just nine. He smiled as he conjured up thoughts of home. "Da place got sweet country rice, fresh catfish, dry monkey meat…"

"Ummmm!" I was getting hungry and he must have been too considering that his first memory was about food.

"Remember when you first come, you didn't know how to speak English!" Curtis chuckled.

I could not help but to join in on the bantering. "Yeah, I come home from school one day and you jumped off da bed yelling '*buaa*'!"

"I not yelling-oh!" He was getting annoyed.

"Yeah you was! Buaa! Buaa! You not able to say hello in English!" By now, Curtis and I were laughing hysterically.

"Well, da only ting dey teach in da village is Mende," Boakai quipped.

I settled down and on a more serious note asked, "How 'bout your ma?" Boakai shared with me before that his mom babbled when she spoke so I wondered how he would communicate with her. According to him, she was not always that way. One day, while walking in the jungle alone, a demonic dwarf stole her voice. Stories of mystical creatures and witchcraft were pretty common in our culture so I believed him.

"Will you be glad to see her?" Curtis joined back into the conversation.

"Yeah!" Boakai replied, with the biggest grin I had seen in a while. Just then, we walked over to one of the street vendors and bought some fried fish and plantains with the money pa had given us. We went back to the motel, ate, bathed and called it a night.

The next morning, we headed out on yet another long and cramped ride. It was extremely hot so we rolled down the windows for some relief. Unfortunately, all we got was hot air mixed with dust. All of our faces were completely red! Along the way, we passed a few towns and villages followed by intermittent periods of dense jungle. At one of the villages, we crossed over a river on a ferry. I was amazed that what appeared to be a wooden raft could carry the weight of all of the people and our car. I was relieved to reach the other side. As the expedition continued, we encountered people when we stopped to stretch, eat and refuel. Other than the language difference, they dressed and seemed just like Liberians. The driver was familiar with the area so he knew where to stop for gas, which was sold alongside the road in one-gallon milk jugs.

We traveled throughout the day and reached Kenema late that afternoon. We were met by soldiers at the border but it was uneventful. Pa paid the driver the remaining half of the fare and we were dropped off at a transportation area. I could not believe that I had been in four different countries over a period of just a few days. I was exhausted but we had to continue by foot to the home of ma's cousins. When we got there, they readily received us. The house was huge with multiple families renting different rooms. Just out the back door was a quaint little courtyard surrounded by small living quarters all attached to the house in the form of a square. While the city had power, the house did not nor did it have running water. The water was retrieved from an outdoor pump conveniently located in the center of the courtyard. Our cousins explained that there was a local refugee program and we needed to go to the United Nations office in order to register. The program assisted newcomers with food such as kidney beans, canned chicken, rice, cooking oil and dehydrated fish. A few days after arriving, we registered and immediately received food.

It was now the beginning of March 1991 and pa decided that we should visit his village to let his family know that we were OK. Prior to the war, he communicated with them via letters but now eight months had gone by without word. Ma decided to stay behind while Beindu and I accompanied pa and Boakai. It was an opportunity for us to meet their side of the family since we had little interaction with them.

We took a small bag of clothing and headed out in a taxi. A few hours later we arrived at a large village called Gegbwema, which sat at the base of the mountain. To pa's surprise, the driver advised that this was as far as he could take us. Apparently the road that used to lead up the mountain to his village was no longer in existence. As such, we needed to trek by foot. Luckily, pa was still familiar with the trails. The one that we took was pretty narrow so we followed each other in a single file line. We spent the afternoon walking uphill with no one else in sight. The jungle surrounded us making it difficult to see anything other than what was straight ahead. The incline was treacherous and everyone breathed heavily. Not having water certainly did not help. Pa ended up having to carry Beindu on his back. It was too much for her to bear.

The sun began to set and the animal noises and rustling in the brush became even more apparent. We were nervous about what lurked nearby so pa told us to pick up the pace. Soon, we ascended into the clouds. It was amazing! I tried to trap some of the billowy whiteness into my bag but to no avail. By twilight, we finally made it to the top.

7 THE VILLAGE

The villagers were one big family that openly worked together and shared resources.

Upon stepping out of the jungle, we immediately entered the Giewahun village. It was a vast open space with sixty or so mud huts spread about. People were engaged in their evening activities. Men were praying on mats while the women cooked on open fires in their outdoor kitchens. As we walked closer, the villagers began to stare. One woman looked at pa and recognized him. She called him by his native name, "Kenny Boakai", and he responded. She started screaming with excitement that he was there. It was like a real-life domino effect. I could literally hear people echoing the message of pa's arrival throughout the village within a matter of seconds. My grandma and other women came out and took off their brightly colored cloth wraps, called lappas, laying them on the ground as a sign of welcome and respect. Soon we were surrounded by hundreds of villagers dancing and singing.

"*O ma ngewo, bise, I wai lo!*" they chanted, thanking God that we had come.

Many stripped their clothing off completely wearing nothing but their loincloths. While it was the best reception I had ever experienced, I must admit that the nudity shocked me. My grandma and others were crying as they hugged pa and lifted us up into their arms.

"*Allah – Akbar*," they exclaimed in Arabic, telling God how great He is.

It had been some four years since my grandma had visited us in Liberia but significantly longer since pa last stepped foot into his village. They all conversed but I could not understand what they were saying. I just smiled and looked on. The most heart-wrenching moment was when Boakai reunited with his mother after five years of living with us. Her high pitch screech rose over the entire group. It was clear that she loved and missed her son more than he could ever know. It was such a joyous occasion!

After the thirty-minute reception, grandma led us to her mud hut. It was square shaped with a porch partially enclosed by a four-foot wall. A door made of interwoven sticks and palm leaves was affixed to the hut with vines. The entrance way was elevated about a foot off the ground so we had to step up and in. Once inside, grandma lit a lantern. The fifteen by fifteen-foot structure was pretty empty with the exception of a large wooden chest that sat in the far left of the room and what appeared to be an oversized mud tub flushed against the wall. Upon further inspection, the tub was a bed filled with hay. We left our bags and headed back outside to the porch. Someone had graciously left a lantern and three tree stumps so grandma motioned for us to sit down. She spread out a mat on the ground and spoke some words to pa in Mende. He translated that a chicken was killed in honor of our arrival and that we would soon be eating. As we waited, the sky blackened, giving way to a sea of stars. They flickered so beautifully across the dark canvas, lighting up the village below. From the top of the mountain, it seemed like I could reach out and grab each and every one of them. It was amazing! The food came and we enjoyed a delicious feast under the observation of smiling onlookers. Soon after, we turned in for the night. I shared the bed with pa and Beindu while grandma spent the night in a neighboring hut.

After about a week, pa decided that he and Beindu would return back to Kenema. Escorted by my two uncles, they headed down the mountain. Boakai and I stayed behind to spend more time with the family. Most of the people in the village did not speak English including my grandma. They mostly communicated with me via hand gestures or relied on Boakai to translate. Although I must say, he also struggled with Mende having not used it in a while. The villagers seemed so appalled by his lack of fluency and mine for that matter. They grumbled, "Ohhhh, Kenny Boakai!" and threw their hands up whenever I looked at them with a blank stare. It was embarrassing and funny all at the same time!

Village life was better than I expected. In fact, it was one of the best times of my life. On a typical day, I woke up to a freshly cooked meal of rice and fish. Soon after, I received a visit from three girls who were all around my age. Although I did not understand what they were saying, I could tell that they were vying for my attention. They giggled a lot as young girls do. I was shy, nervous and excited. After hanging out with them, I accompanied my grandma to her farm to dig up cassava, check on the rice plants and drive off scavengers. We also gathered nuts from the palm trees to make palm oil. This was used a lot for cooking. Occasionally, we set and emptied fish traps.

When not in the jungle, I hung out in the village. Because I was a visitor, the people were extremely hospitable and generous. They gave me gifts like food and clothing. Each evening, I went to the mosque to pray with grandma. She did not force me to go, but I did so out of respect and because that was what everyone else did. She seemed very happy and proud of me. Sometimes in the evening when the sun cooled down, kids were sent two miles into the jungle to get water from a water hole. They were also responsible for keeping the fire burning. I tagged along and observed. The villagers were one big family that openly worked together and shared resources.

By the end of March 1991 it was Ramadan, a time of fasting and prayer followed by feasting. Each evening at 6:00 p.m., every household prepared a meal and gathered at the mosque for prayer. Afterwards, we sat on mats on the ground and partook of the food with our bare hands.

Before long, I became acclimated to life in the village. I spoke some Mende and even took it upon myself to sit in the back of the school house. Classes started early in the morning with recitation. Each age group had their own assignment so altogether it sounded like a chaotic all-male choir. The conductor, dressed in traditional Muslim attire, walked about with his hands braced behind his back. Even his massive beard could not detract from his stern facial expression. His trained ear quickly identified when someone messed up. Without a word, he whipped out the long stick from behind his back and struck the offender across the head. They tried to take cover but were no match for his speed. It was understood by the students that the performance was never to be interrupted by tears. As quickly as the attack ensued, the recipient joined back in where he left off.

Soon I learned how to read and write some of the Arabic language. It looked like an extra fancy version of cursive. Getting used to writing right to left was tricky. People started looking at me as a member of the village instead of a visitor. This meant increasing my workload to the level of the other kids. One of my uncles constantly teased me by calling me a "city boy". He said that I looked weak and made it his mission to toughen me up! In addition to my regular duties, he took me to his farm to clear the brush and dig for cassava roots a few times per week. It was hard work but I never complained.

Being out and about in the elements, I eventually caught malaria and suffered from high fever, vomiting and diarrhea. Luckily, there was a village nurse who was trained in modern medicine. She treated me with a regimen of shots and oral medications, just as ma had when I caught malaria back home in Liberia. I actually did not mind needles, it was the pills that I hated. The bitter taste of the chloroquine tablets made me gag. Nevertheless, I complied. After the shot was administered, the nurse gave grandma care instructions and asked that I return for additional treatment. Within a few weeks I was better.

Not long after my recovery, I was running in the jungle and a sharp stick pierced my foot. Rather than worry grandma, I plugged my wound with mud. Before long, infection set in and I limped with a swollen foot. When grandma finally discovered it, she was very upset. She took me back to the nurse for treatment and it was then that I first saw Vyrette, the nurse's daughter.

"Hello," I said, as I awkwardly leaned from my seat trying to peer around grandma. She stood blocking my full view of one of the most beautiful creatures that I had ever seen. Vyrette's dark mocha skin was sheer perfection without a blemish in sight. Her short natural hair accented her perfectly chiseled jawline and slender shoulders. She stood towards the back of the hut folding clothes wearing a burgundy printed lappa tied at the neck. I assumed that her task distracted her from hearing my greeting so I tried again. "Hello."

By now grandma glanced down at me with a squint of curiosity, quickly followed by a grin and a step to the side.

I guess it was pretty obvious.

"*Buaa*," Vyrette replied saying hello. Her full defined lips parted slowly as she smiled exposing her pearly white teeth. Just then, her ma returned with the antibiotic. Vyrette excused herself and I was asked to stand up and drop my shorts. I did so, all the while thankful that I only had to expose my butt to the two women!

The next day, a few of us boys were headed down to the water hole when out of the brush Vyrette emerged in her topless glory. She carried a bucket of water on her head. Suddenly an uncontrollable urge came over me, so I ran up and squeezed her supple breasts! She grinned and continued walking while the onlookers cheered. I felt like a king! I wanted Vyrette to be my girlfriend but later found out that she was arranged to marry Boakai's brother. I was crushed. I heard of arranged marriages before, but never had a person close to me participate. I remembered seeing this couple in Kenema. The girl was around thirteen and her husband, a relative, was in his fifties. I commented to pa that it was weird. He explained that it was not weird and actually smart to marry in the family. Not only did it preserve wealth and possessions, but family could also be trusted more so than a stranger. I still did not understand it but could now see why he felt the way that he did.

One night, I joined the villagers at an evening fire. As we sat, the conversation came up about the Revolutionary United Front (RUF), a rebel force that had formed in Sierra Leone. Many of the villagers were adamant that no rebel force could overpower the Sierra Leonean army. I spoke up about the killings that I witnessed by the National Patriotic Front of Liberia (NPFL) and warned that the RUF would be no different. Many laughed and brushed off my account as being over exaggerated by my youthfulness but within a week they too would see for themselves.

Someone came running up the mountain screaming that there was a rebel sighting. The message got around and soon everyone gathered at the mosque. Night was quickly approaching so it was decided that we should get a few belongings and head into the jungle. It seemed like déjà vu, seeing the trail of hundreds of villagers fleeing from their homes under the light of scattered lanterns. My heart raced at the thought of what might be coming. We cowered amongst the bushes for hours with no sign of rebel forces. Soon the elders decided that we should turn back. My grandma was reluctant but obliged. Over the next few days, the rumors continued to circulate. Soon pa showed up and said that he too heard about the rebel upheaval. He said that we had to leave at first light.

Early the next morning we headed out carrying a bag and food that grandma prepared for the road. She wept as if it would be the last time that we would see one another. None of us were certain. Before leaving, pa put money into a plastic bag and buried it in the middle of her hut. There was no need inquiring if grandma was coming with us. There was no way that she was leaving the village. It was a part of her and everyone else for that matter. Even my adopted brother, Boakai, decided that it was time for him to return to his birthplace. His ma begged him to leave but he refused. Pa honored his wishes. While I was certainly going to miss him, I realized that I would have done the same thing. With that, we said our goodbyes and my uncle escorted us down the mountain. Once we got to the bottom, we found that there was no longer transportation available. A lot of people took off once they heard rumors about the RUF. We had no other choice but to take the thirty mile walk back to Kenema.

The trip took all day traveling along the Bo-Kenema Highway passing through several small villages. There was no one in sight. We mostly walked in silence stopping along the way to eat some of the rice grandma sent and to drink from streams. My feet had swollen in my sandals but I never complained. By evening, we made it to the house.

Ma was relieved that we were safe and insisted that we depart as soon as possible.

8 VOYAGE

The once peaceful and serene ocean transformed into roaring rapids.

The next morning, we bid farewell to everyone and caught a taxi forty-three miles to a relative's house in Bo. Bo was the second largest city in Sierra Leone and was heading away from the rumored rebel sightings. By the time we were dropped off by the taxi and walked some five miles to the house, it was afternoon. The house had several rooms rented to different families. Our group of six shared a room. Since there was no refugee agency, we lived off of the money that pa brought with him.

While in Bo, the Muslim customs became even more apparent. Mostly everyone dressed in traditional wear and there was a huge mosque in the center of the community. Prayers echoed over loud speakers throughout the day. A lot of the time, we explored the nearby area or just sat around. There were a ton of kids in the house. Luckily for me, I had picked up some Krio while staying in Kenema so I was able to communicate with my newfound friends. Many of them attended school, so I anxiously awaited their return each day. With all of the teenage girls in the house, my raging hormones continued to have their way but not without consequence. One day, a girl's father caught us dry humping. He was so angry that he immediately reported me to ma. She became very defensive and asserted that I was being targeted for being Liberian. Not only did ma say that I was too young to have sex but she said that my penis was entirely too small. To further prove her point, she pulled down my pants and exposed my privates for the whole world to see! I was so humiliated! Needless to say, I was glad when our one-month stint there came to an end.

Our next move took us 149 miles west to another relative's place in Freetown. Since it was the capital city, pa thought that it would offer a better opportunity. Upon arrival, we were met by a landlord who told us that our relative didn't actually own the house, but rather rented a room from him. Since he was not there, the landlord did not allow us to come inside so we sat on the porch most of the day. The more we waited, the more agitated he became. He kept spitting and sweeping dirt in our direction. At one point, his wife brought his meal outside and he started eating. It smelled amazing! I was so hungry that I could not help but stare. The other children did the same in hopes that he would offer us some food. This upset him even more so he started making indirect comments about refugees taking over the country. After a while, ma addressed him head on about his rude commentary. They were both yelling and there was nothing that pa could do to get the situation under control! *MMP on the Attack,* I thought. The next thing I knew, the landlord ordered us off his property.

As we gathered our stuff and started walking away, a

Liberian passerby noticed ma's accent and asked if we were OK. She explained the situation to him and he said that there was a ship at the dock scheduled to leave for Liberia the next morning. According to him, the United Nations contracted with the shipping company to transport refugees back to Liberia. The man walked with us a few miles to the port. Once there, security guards asked if we were Liberian refugees and allowed us to come in. We were excited to have stumbled upon this opportunity at a time when we needed it most.

It was late in the evening so we were given a flashlight and led through the concrete maze crowded with cargo containers. While most of the area was black, I could see some light coming from the two ships that docked nearby and another that sat in the distance. The pier itself stretched on for miles. About thirty feet from the water, the guard stopped and opened a cargo container, which looked similar to the back of a tractor trailer. He told us that we could sleep there for the night. It was half stocked with goods so we took it upon ourselves to rip the plastic and sneak a few cans of sardines. Not too long after we settled in, a few other families joined our group bringing the total to twenty-one people. The fit was very tight so some of us slept on top of the packages while others laid on the wooden surface. Ironically, with the cool ocean breeze, the steady humming from the nearby ships and the sound of the water hitting the dock, it was one of the most relaxing nights of sleep that I had in a long time.

The next morning, I was able to get a better view of the port. We were actually towards the end of the dock. Looking out into the Atlantic, I could see a retention wall of rocks. They seemed strategically placed, creating a passageway leading into the port. Just beyond the rocks were shipping lanes with various size boats and ships passing by. Every so often, the sound of long drawn out horns echoed in my ears like a tuba. The water itself looked dirty and foam gathered near the dock. The stench of fish quickly pierced my nose.

The crowd started to grow throughout the morning. It was mostly women and children, who like us, carried minimal belongings. From their accents, they sounded Liberian. I watched as they gathered waiting for the ship to arrive. I wondered what they had gone through leading up to this point and if they had a plan. I looked at my own parents and wondered what our plan entailed. *Where would we go? Did our house still stand?*

Another loud horn rang out and I noticed a rusty white feeder ship with blue lettering backing into the dock. I marveled at the sheer size of the vessel and the hundreds of colorful cargo containers that were stacked on top. *Was this our ship!* It must have been because the security guards ordered the crowd to step back. We waited and waited and were eventually told that the departure time was not until the following day. We were all disappointed and had no choice but to wait. That night, additional containers were made available to nearly one hundred refugees.

The next morning, people lined up so we joined them. I was eager to set sail. I imagined myself on the top deck, taking in all of the beautiful sights. By the time they finally dropped the stern ramp and permitted us to board the ship, it was afternoon. I was so annoyed. The crew members led us upstairs to the exterior passageway and we departed around 4:00 p.m. There was no safety briefing. The only instruction we received was to keep our belongings with us and to anticipate arriving into Monrovia the following morning.

The ship pulled out slowly and I immediately broke free from our group and headed up a few stairs to the main deck. I found a spot to myself and looked out at the ocean. The horn sounded several times as we cleared the port. Small fishing boats passed by heading back to shore. The view of Freetown was absolutely stunning. The mountains continued as far as the eye could see. A few other onlookers and my brother Curtis joined me on the deck. Everyone was excited.

Once we hit the open waters, the wind picked up. The temperature quickly fell as the sun set so Curtis and I decided to head back downstairs with the others. Under the dim lighting of the passageway, families huddled together to keep warm. Some covered themselves with sheets and lappas while others endured the chill. I was surprised by how cold it was.

Several hours into the trip, the ocean became rough rocking the ship from side to side. Massive waves toppled over into the passageway as the vessel lifted up and slammed back down to the surface. Everyone was terrified and I was certain that the ship would capsize. My family hovered together as far away as we could from the openings running alongside the ship. Others did the same but it was of no use, the water continued to splash in. It was hard to believe that the once peaceful and serene ocean transformed into roaring rapids. Not being able to see the raging beast made it even more terrifying. The expressions on the faces of the people morphed from fear to painstaking agony. Before long, someone vomited and it started a chain reaction. In a matter of seconds, Pa dashed to the side of the ship and hurled...then Beindu then Curtis then Peter. It was disgusting! I was queasy but managed to hold it in. Needless to say, it was a horrible night with no sleep. By early morning, we docked in Monrovia, Liberia.

9 HOME AGAIN

Everything that my parents had worked for was gone.

It was June 1991, nearly a year since we were driven out of our home. Stepping off the ship at the Freeport of Monrovia, we knew nothing about what Liberia had become or if our house still stood. One thing was for sure, the ECOMOG soldiers had a very visible presence. They were all over the port, dressed in green uniforms with the green and white Nigerian flag encrusted on their "ECOMOG" sleeve patch. Some stood stationed at posts surrounded by sandbag walls while others manned the battleships docked at the port. All were armed with FN FAL semi-automatic rifles.

We walked amongst a group of passengers towards the port exit. As we neared a gate, pa told us to wait inside while he took a taxi to Gardnersville, a suburb of Monrovia, to see if his relatives still lived nearby. He figured that would be a better option than going straight home because we did not know if our house still stood. As he disappeared out of the gate, the ECOMOG soldiers searched the few people that were coming in. Most appeared to be workers. As we waited on the bench, my stomach pinched with hunger. We had not eaten since leaving Freetown. I heard the sounds of voices and vehicles coming from the other side of the concrete wall. I imagined that there was food for sale just beyond the gate. How I wished we could go and buy some fried fish and plantains.

Pa returned and his look said it all! His relatives were still alive so we had a place to stay! We all headed through the checkpoint and jumped into the taxi. As we drove down Somalia Drive, I could not help but to stare out the window at the country that I called home. She was still standing but showed visible signs of being tortured. Buildings were diminished to ash, vehicles were overturned and most things were covered with bullet holes. It was a sight to see. We traveled six miles passing nothing but destruction. The silence in the vehicle and the gasps said it all. We were in disbelief and felt blessed to be alive.

The driver dropped us off at the Gardnersville Supermarket and we continued by foot to my uncle's place in the town of Chocolate City about a mile away. I had never been there before, but heard that it got its name from the enormous mud accumulation during the rainy season. As we walked, the ground became very sandy and I noticed something strange. There were millions of fire ants crawling about everywhere. It was so bad that every few steps someone complained about a bite and smacked the critters off their skin. We were like a drill team marching with our knees in a high quickstep motion.

I was so relieved when we made it to the house, which sat on a hill near the edge of a mangrove swamp. The front was risen up by concrete pillars so that water could pass under it during high tide. We were greeted by my uncle's two widows. Apparently, he perished during the war leaving behind the women, their two children, two grandchildren and his brother. Ma asked my aunts why there were so many ants and they said that they came during the war because of the number of dead bodies lying around. We were shown to our room and settled in for the night.

The next day, pa, Curtis and I caught a taxi six miles to the Red Light area in Monrovia. Once there, we walked a couple of miles on the Monrovia-Kakata Highway to our neighborhood. We passed through several military checkpoints with more Nigerian ECOMOG soldiers and armored trucks. As we turned off on the dirt road heading into our neighborhood, it was clear that the area had been abandoned for some time. The road was battered by overgrown grass and rain erosion. While a few neighbors had cleared their yards, for the most part the jungle took over everything including our house. It was hardly recognizable through the brush, which in some areas grew more than six feet tall. We borrowed machetes from a neighbor and chopped a pathway from the main road some fifty yards to our front door, which sat halfway open. As we made our entrance, we could see that bullet holes allowed for glimpses of light to pass into the living room. We searched the house and found that it had been completely gutted. You name it...clothing, beds, furniture, pictures...all of it was taken. I sat down on the floor in disbelief. Curtis joined me hanging his head. When I glanced up at pa, I noticed for the first time ever that tears filled his eyes. I couldn't imagine how he must have felt. Everything that he and ma had worked for was gone. He never let the pain overtake him. He held the floodgates and with solace said that we should be happy to have our lives.

We headed out the back door to find even more devastation. In addition to the brush, there were explosives all over the yard. We saw everything from grenades and mortar shells to undetonated RPG shells with the tips still stuck in the ground. We took care as we stepped around them and decided that we had seen enough for one day. Before leaving, we returned the machetes and bid farewell to the neighbors.

Back in Chocolate City, life started all over again. Schools were open but we could not afford to pay tuition for everyone. Pa spent most days reading while ma returned back to work at the JFK Medical Center as a nurse. I spent a lot of time exploring the swamp. I was in awe of the abundance of tilapia that swam so closely to the house. There were also a lot of ugly mudskipper fish that everyone avoided. They looked like a strange combination of a catfish and a frog. Somehow they managed to breathe for significant periods of time outside of the water.

Next to the main house was an outhouse. Unlike those that I had seen before, this one was designed so that the waste dropped directly into the water. Curtis explained that the fish ate the waste. I was disgusted by the thought of catching fish that had eaten someone's poop or my own for that matter. I convinced Curtis that we should fish deeper into the swamp. The problem was the further we walked, the more the smell of must and decayed mud intensified. To make matters worse, the swamp seemed to attract every type of insect, all of whom were on steroids just waiting for an opportunity to feast on us. Snakes, of varying species, were in abundance. Assuming that they were all poisonous, we avoided them. The mangrove trees were an annoyance with their intertwining roots making it very difficult to pass by. Depending on the tide, the terrain changed so it was challenging to retrace our steps. As such, we learned to manage our fishing trips around the tide.

Over a period of time, it became evident that the fish were smart. Most of our catch was small because the bigger fish remained near their food source, which unfortunately was the outhouse. Soon, I overcame my hesitance and we fished near the house. We used hardened cornmeal as bait because we figured that it resembled human waste. Before consuming the fish, we cleaned and soaked them in lime juice. Our catch was so plentiful that we sold the surplus at the local market for ten Liberian dollars (LRD) per five fish or what was equivalent to $0.12 USD. Obviously, we were not in it for the money. We used our proceeds to buy supplies and candy.

One day, a customer returned after having bought our fish the day prior. "Back so soon!" I smiled in hopes that she would buy again.

She shook her head and turned up her mouth in disgust dismissing my inquiry. As she walked away, Curtis and I looked at each other. We knew exactly what she meant. We quickly packed up for fear that she would spread the word about our shitty fish! Nevertheless, we did not let it deter us from returning to the marketplace to sell again and again.

The swamp became our playground and fishing was our favorite attraction. Well, that was until we came across some guys casting a net into the water. We walked over to them and asked what they were doing. They explained that they were catching crabs. They not only taught us the technique for catching them, but also showed us how to build crab traps. With the exception of a few pinches here and there, crabbing seemed a lot easier than fishing. It was also great to have a different type of meat for a change.

One evening Curtis and I were catching so many crabs that we had forgotten all about the tide coming in. By the time we realized, the water had already reached knee level.

"Oh shit!" Curtis screamed. "We got to go!"

In a panic, we desperately tried to retrace our steps through the muddy water, but it was of no use. What usually was walkable ground with visible mud pits was now completely covered over by water disguising all evidence of danger. We were lost in a web of mangrove trees with moving water steadily rising. My heart raced as I trailed closely behind Curtis carrying a rice bag full of our supplies and the crabs that we caught. He was a swimmer so I figured that if need be he could save me. As we carefully stepped through the water, Curtis poked the ground with a long stick that he carried trying to avoid sinkholes and other hidden obstacles. Despite his best efforts, we both lost our footing on a few occasions tripping over mangrove roots.

"I tink it's dis way," he said, pointing to a clearing about fifty yards ahead. We turned in that direction and suddenly Curtis fell through the mud. In a matter of seconds, it reached his chest. "Help me! Help me BK, help me!" he screamed. His face was overrun with terror.

I dropped the bag and stepped towards him extending my arm as far as I could without risking stepping into the hole. He desperately tried to grab my hand but could not reach me. The more he struggled, the more he sunk. He gasped for air going into a full fledge panic attack.

I knew that I had to react quickly. I looked down and noticed his long stick floating in the water. I picked it up and reached out to him with it. Curtis grabbed ahold of it and the endless battle of tug of war begun. The more I pulled, the more the monstrous mud pit fought to consume him. That, coupled with his body weight, was overpowering. I was exhausted.

"Help!" I cried out, but we were so deep in the swamp that no one heard us. I knew that I was his only hope for survival and was determined not to give up. I switched my stance to get the best grip. I tugged with all of my might. Soon I was able to pull him close enough to grab his hands and drag him out. His head was under the water momentarily but he quickly rose to his feet. We were both out of breath but turned our attention to finding our way out. We grabbed the stick once more and continued maneuvering through the mangrove trees until we made our way back home. We laid low on going deep into the swamp for a while but eventually returned.

After a month of being back in Liberia, we decided to spend the weekends fixing up our house. We used machetes to finish clearing the brush from the outside and then tackled the interior cleaning and repairs. The whole process took about six months but we were glad to be back in our old neighborhood. Word spread about our return so soon we reunited with my older brother, Francis and sister, Mariama, who were doing well and living in the downtown area. My brothers, Opa and Opi, who parted ways with us in Kakata, also returned home.

In addition to working at the hospital, ma opened a small clinic and drugstore in Gardnersville. She employed a prior co-worker to cover the shop whenever she had to report to work. Ma treated patients and even delivered babies in the back room. She was back to the glory of her Voice of America days, gaining popularity through word of mouth and her willingness to barter. Through her connections at JFK Hospital, she was able to buy medicine in bulk and resell it in the drugstore. I was proud of the way that she started her own business and helped the community.

ECOMOG soldiers continued to canvas the whole area. There were thousands with reinforcements steadily coming. Some of the soldiers lived in the neighborhood homes that were still abandoned. Ma decided that it would be in our best interest to open up our home to the soldiers as well. She voluntarily went by the command post and within a week we had two men living with us. They mostly stayed to themselves only coming in to sleep. Even still, it was comforting to feel like we were under their protection.

The effects of war remained evident as the country was left with no power or running water. As such, we kept two

50 gallon barrels on the outside of the house to catch rainwater for washing clothes and bathing. Inside, there was a hundred-gallon barrel that we replenished with well water for drinking and cooking. The nearest well was about three miles away, so every few days all of us boys made multiple trips carrying five-gallon containers.

In an effort to be more efficient, pa decided that we should dig our own well. We knew that it would be a very challenging task because our land was mostly soft red clay filled with rocks and very large boulders. After several attempts, we finally found a good spot. All of the boys pitched in to dig using shovels, our hands and various tools. As the well deepened, we used a bucket attached to a string to hoist up the dirt. Steps were carved into the sides of the walls about a foot apart to climb in and out. Every so often, we alternated jobs so that everyone stayed fresh.

By day three, we made significant progress and the well was about four feet wide by twenty feet deep. The person who dug inside the bottom of the well was barely visible from the top. Luckily, it held a stable form without collapsing. Not long after I started digging inside the well on day four, the dirt became muddy and splashed in my eye. As I wiped my face, I yelled up to my brothers that I hit water. They yelled back down that it was too soon. Before I could say anything else, cold water covered my bare feet and crept up my leg.

"It coming!" I screamed, as I quickly placed my foot in the step closest to me. I shifted my body weight reaching for the step above me and my foot broke right through. I'm not sure if it was because my foot was wet or the water loosened the dirt but I knew that I was in trouble. The water was coming in fast and I thought that I would drown. "Help!" I screeched, but there was nothing that anyone could do but tell me to climb. I found my footing in another step and dug in to brace myself with each movement. My nerves got the best of me and I could feel sweat pouring from my armpits down my bare side. I tried not to look down only focusing on the light above hoping to outrun the water. When I got within reach of my brothers, they yanked me out. I let out a sigh of relief happy to have missed such a close call. Within a few minutes the well was filled with water. I could not believe that we had accomplished such a feat! The water was muddy so pa told us to cover it up with tin and wait for the dirt to settle before boiling and drinking it.

Similar to before the war, there was no formal system for waste management. We continued using our outhouse and underground septic tank. We dug small holes to discard trash. If one spot filled up, we simply made another one. Most of our waste was biodegradable so it never really accumulated. It also provided nutrients to the soil so we decided to start a farm using an acre of land near the house. Since pa grew up in the village, he was an experienced farmer. I too had picked up a few tips from my time there. He put all of us boys to work tilling the land and planting crops. When it came time for watering, we made trips to the well and filled containers. The process was a lot of hard work but ultimately we were able to grow peanuts, corn, sweet potatoes, tomatoes, peppers, onions and cassava. Many nights the animals came and ate the plants. In order to protect our crops, we fenced the entire farm by intertwining sticks and vines. We used noisemakers to scare off birds. Homemade traps were placed at each entrance for animals who managed to find their way in. Catching them was an additional bonus!

After establishing the farm, ma enrolled us back in school with the extra money that was coming in from the store. It had been over two years since I last attended so I was reluctant to go. I returned to the sixth grade with an afternoon class time. I spent the mornings doing chores and preparing meals.

Liberia was nowhere near stable. An interim

government was established in the capital city of Monrovia but the majority of the country was still under rebel control. For security, the Monrovian government established a curfew stating that only military personnel could be on the streets between 6:00 p.m. and 6:00 a.m. Anyone who broke the curfew could be arrested or shot on sight. This meant that when school let out, I had to hustle to make the two-mile trip back home. Most times my friend and I ran and took short cuts using back roads. Yet and still there were a few times when we missed curfew. Luckily, we were never caught.

The hard work on the farm paid off. With the exception of rice and some meats, we were pretty self-sufficient. We ate fresh foods daily and decided to expand to the other side of our land. The problem was that we still had not cleared that particular area, so the threat of dangerous explosives lurked in the brush. With caution, we decided to move forward with the expansion. One day, Opa and I noticed a balled up blanket. Upon closer inspection, we found two AK-47 assault rifles and two magazines filled with ammunition. We ran home and told ma and she reported it to one of the ECOMOG soldiers. He took it and warned us not to touch any weapons and to avoid lighting fires.

About a week later, Opa and I were back outside clearing the brush. After piling some of it up, he set it on fire. We continued cutting with our machetes tossing the scraps into the blaze as we went along. Smoke quickly filled the air. Before long, we noticed two armed ECOMOG soldiers walking across our property headed in our direction. One had his rifle on his back while the other held his at his side with the barrel pointing down. Opa shot me a puzzled look and I shrugged my shoulders because I was just as stumped as he was. We continued working as they approached.

"PUT – THE – FIRE – OUT!" one soldier said matter-of-factly.

We quickly picked up the shovels laying nearby tossing dirt on the fire. *What did we do?* I wondered, as we continued to smother the blaze.

"Come with us."

Opa and I responded by dropping the shovels and following the two men. As we walked in silence, my mind flashed back to the warning we were given the prior week. I felt awful that my memory lapse had gotten us in trouble. As we headed down the trail, I could see the ECOMOG headquarters. They had taken over the largest and most beautiful house in the community previously owned by a prominent business man. I had only been inside of the 20-foot concrete fence topped with barbed wire one time when the owner hosted a community party. Unfortunately, all of guests remained outdoors so all I could do was marvel at the beautiful, white castle that served as the showpiece of the property.

As we walked, one of the soldiers kept looking back at me as if he felt sorry for me. It was the same look that ma gave every time I was about to get spanked by pa. I could tell that she wanted to say or do something but for whatever reason did not.

"Stop," the soldier said. "How old are you?"

"I thirteen," I responded.

"Go back home."

Apparently he gave into whatever was pulling at him. The other soldier just turned away motioning Opa to follow him. I immediately turned and started running back home. I figured they were going to throw Opa in jail so I knew that I needed to tell ma quickly. All I could think about were the stories that I heard about the notorious prison Bella Yella. *Would my brother be tortured?* I thought, as I picked up the pace. Within a few minutes I heard a blood curdling scream unlike anything that I had ever heard before. It continued on and on and seemed to amplify as if it were over a loudspeaker. It was Opa. He was begging for mercy.

"*Oga*-ohhhhh!!!" he screamed. The word "oga" was a Nigerian term for "boss" signifying respect. "Please-ohhhhh! I beg you-ohhhhh! I will not do it again-ohhhhh!"

My worst fears came to pass so I ran as fast as I could. When I reached the house ma and two of her cousins were sitting outside under the tree. I raced to her barely able to catch my breath.

"What happen?" she asked, clearly seeing that something was wrong.

"Opa...da soldier beating Opa at headquarters," I managed to get out.

The women and my brother Opi quickly followed me down the path that not too long ago was overtaken by the sounds of Opa's screams. Now all that could be heard was the chirping of birds and the occasional military truck. *Did this mean that...?* I could not bear the thought.

As we reached the clearing, we saw Opa heading our way so we hurried to meet him. He walked with his head down and his t-shirt in his hand. He was sobbing uncontrollably. I had never seen a man cry so hard. Ma asked what happened but the welts and lacerations all over his chest and back clearly told the story.

In between his tears and sniffling, he went on a rant that was barely coherent. "Dey will die! I hope all of dem go to the frontline and die!" I wanted to laugh but it was neither the time nor place. In the coming days, however, he became the butt of all of our jokes.

By October 1992, I continued to go to school in the afternoon. I was in the seventh grade and struggled as usual. Math was incomprehensible and I retained the reading and spelling lessons just enough to pass the test. After that, it all went out of the window but that never deterred me from trying. I continued to spend most of my free time fishing. My days at the swamp left a lasting impression that I wanted to share with my brothers. One day, Opa, Opi and I headed into the jungle to find rattan to make fishing baskets. These slender, vine-like stems were good for weaving. About three miles into our walk, we ran into an ECOMOG checkpoint along the trail. It was outfitted with a small hut structure with a few chairs and small table inside. Stationed there, were three armed Nigerian soldiers. The sound of talking could be heard coming across the open line of the walkie-talkie. Noticing Opa's machete, they asked what we were doing. He explained and we were allowed to pass easily.

"Why dey all da way out here?" I asked my brothers.

"I don' know," Opa responded.

We brushed it off and continued walking on the path looking for rattan. We could not find any so we ventured deeper into the forest. About a half a mile later, we noticed yet another checkpoint ahead. This one was different, yet familiar. There was a single rope blocking the path with three red rags hanging on it. I immediately had flashbacks of my walk through hell! From the shocked looks on my brother's faces, they too felt the same but it was too late to turn around.

"Why dey here?" Opi whispered.

"Shuttttttttt up!" Opa warned, trying not to move his lips like a ventriloquist.

Before we knew it, we were being approached by a rebel soldier. He was around thirty years old, thin and dark skinned wearing a sleeveless dashiki and a pair of dirty denim jeans tucked into his combat boots. He casually strolled over taking a puff from a joint with his AK-47 strapped to his chest.

"Wha' ya'll doin' here?" he asked.

"Jus' looking for rattan," Opa replied. The soldier nodded his head acknowledging what my brother said and continued puffing away. The flowery opium smell filled the air. There were three more soldiers there but they just glanced over seemingly unfazed by our presence. Their rifles laid nearby on the table.

"Ya'll know we were here?" the soldier asked.

As not to alarm him, Opa lied, "Yeah, we know."

"I da captain here," he said with arrogance. "I can't let all ya'll go. Let da lil boy stay here." He pointed to a bench. My brothers walked off and I told myself not to show fear. *Just keep smiling,* I thought. All the while, I was petrified and angry with the ECOMOG soldiers for not warning us about the potential danger.

The rebels seemed like any other group of friends. They talked amongst themselves and played cards. Some drank while others smoked. Although they never spoke a word to me, my heart pounded each minute that I spent waiting on that bench. Soon, my brothers returned and said they could not find what they were looking for. We thanked the soldiers and quickly hurried on our way. Back home, we told everyone about what we saw. While people were afraid, they felt that the rebels did not pose an immediate threat because of the cease fire agreement and the strong ECOMOG presence. Boy, were they wrong!

10 OCTOBER OCTOPUS

Like tentacles, the attack spanned in every direction across the city.

Our neighborhood had grown significantly over the prior months with several of our neighbors hosting groups of men. Mr. Wallace, who worked with pa for as long as I could remember, had six new housemates. The other neighbor down the hill hosted four and so on and so forth. It was all kind of strange. Even more peculiar was the fact that the new residents had a ton of visitors. Ma long suspected that the newcomers were rebel soldiers on a recon mission. We brushed it off and asked that she keep her thoughts to herself. The last thing that we needed was to create tension with the people around us.

On October 15, gunfire rang out. We ran into the house and took cover. While the fighting was not in our immediate neighborhood, we could tell that it was nearby. After an hour or so, the shooting ceased and we came out of the house. The ECOMOG soldier, who lived next door, explained that they were attacked by a small unit of rebels but were able to push them back into the forest. He said that they would remain on high alert but believed that the situation was contained. One thing was for sure, the cease fire agreement had been broken. My parents decided that we should no longer go to school and that ma would not return to work until things blew over. Unlike the last time, they did not want us separated.

Over the next week, the fighting escalated and shooting could be heard all day and night. We hardly slept as tracer rounds lit up the black sky. They looked like red and green shooting stars. It was eerily beautiful. Other than a quick scurry to fetch water or food, we rarely left the house. In the moments that we did, it was amazing to witness ECOMOG soldiers posted in fox holes and behind heavy machine guns. They seemed so skilled in weaponry and tactics, yet the rebel forces had strength in numbers and a willingness to die. The more the ECOMOG fended off the rebels, the more they attacked. The operation was referred to as *Operation Octopus,* perhaps because like tentacles, it spanned in every direction across the city.

The thought of having to flee our home again after all of the hard work that it took to rebuild it was unbearable. Nevertheless, the fighting intensified so much by the end of the second week that it was no longer safe to remain in the area. I was on edge jumping at every sound.

BOOM! BOOM! The ground literally shook each time a rocket hit. The dishes in the old wooden cabinet in our kitchen rattled uncontrollably. We scurried to pack a few bags and headed out at first light. We stopped by some of the neighbor's houses to see where they intended to go. To our dismay, there were no responses. In fact, the whole neighborhood looked like a ghost town. I could tell that my parents regretted not leaving sooner.

"Hurry!" pa said ushering everyone towards Monrovia-

Kakata Highway.

We walked for a quarter mile remaining on guard as the sounds of shooting and explosions rang out constantly. Just up ahead, the road began to incline. On top of the hill was a group of ten soldiers clustered together, back to back in battle formation. Every so often, they let off shots into the woods. As we came closer, two soldiers broke formation walking quickly towards us while still on guard.

"Why are you here! Make haste!" one of the soldiers shouted, waving at us to keep going up the hill.

We started speed walking trying to keep hold of the few belongings that we carried. I could not believe that this was happening right here and right now. *What about the ECOMOG control of the area?* I felt like we had been misled into letting our guard down.

We decided to head to Gardnersville, the place where we lived when we first returned to Liberia. As we traveled down the road, the seemingly deserted area turned into a sea of panicked people swarming about trying to flee. It was utter chaos! Pa told us to stay close and keep moving. ECOMOG soldiers lined both sides of the highway firing tank rounds and field artillery.

BOOM! BOOM! We ducked and took cover as an onslaught of rounds released overhead. The soldiers were so tactical moving together swiftly like a school of fish. Each man covered the other.

BOOM! The ground trembled beneath my feet and smoke engulfed the atmosphere. Each explosion was quickly followed by the sound of a shell zipping through the air followed by a distant explosion. Everything stood still and I wondered who was on the other side of the impact. I mean, I knew that they were targeting rebel forces but what about the people, who just like us, were trying to get out of harm's way. I looked around at the faces. Most showed fear. People cowered and clung on to their loved ones. The Senegalese contingent, on the other hand, towered in stature and prowess. They maintained focus on the mission at hand. Their ebony faces remained stern and they constantly maneuvered about preparing for the next move. For a moment, I got lost in their precision. I imagined myself as one of them, clad in camouflage, toting a FAMAS assault rifle and defending my city. It felt like I was in a real life action movie. We continued another five miles towards Gardnersville taking cover as needed. The further we traveled, the more distant the fighting became. We were grateful when we made it to ma's drugstore. Although small, all eight of us managed through the night by sleeping in between the aisles on the concrete floor.

The next day, Opa and Opi once again decided that they were going to stay with some friends in downtown Monrovia. Ma was very angry about their decision to part ways. As they walked away with backpacks in tow, she yelled that they were making a big mistake and that our family needed to stick together. They never acknowledged her and just kept walking. I felt a tear slide down my cheek. I had just welcomed my brothers back home a few months prior. It was too much to think about.

Being in Gardnersville was unsettling. We remained on high alert as rebel forces continued to push towards the capital city of Monrovia. Heavy artillery could be heard throughout the day and night. Tanks roamed the streets as did armed soldiers. The curfew was still in effect so we spent most of our time cramped inside of the drugstore. The heat was unbearable because ma insisted that the doors remain locked and the windows closed. On the third day, we were awakened by heavy gunfire. We came out to see what was happening and there were hundreds of people walking down the street heading towards downtown Monrovia. Ma asked someone why everyone was leaving and they said that the rebels were nearby. Not taking any chances, we gathered a few items and joined the group on the five-mile journey to Monrovia. With each passing minute, it seemed like the sound of gunfire drew closer. However, we never saw anyone engaging, just soldiers holding their positions in anticipation of what was to come. We alternated between walking and running, mostly in silence, as did the rest of the group. In about three hours, we came to the Johnson Street Bridge, which was one of two bridges leading into the heart of Monrovia. The two-lane concrete structure was visibly aged and molded. From its peak, I could see Bushrod Island, a popular entertainment destination surrounded by the Montserrado River. A walkway led from the top of the bridge down to the small island, which boosted an amphitheater, decorated with traditional African murals. Massive palm and coconut trees spread throughout the landscape and a rocky embankment surrounded the entire island. My uncle took me there once for a dance performance in celebration of culture day. This was a day when different tribes came together in unity to celebrate our unique customs. It was really nice. A far cry from where we were now. Looking out to the left, I could see the Montserrado River swirling in and out of the surrounding swamp like a Chinese dragon. It brought back memories of Gardnersville and my swamp adventures with my brother Curtis. Those were the days!

Although there were no cars, everyone stayed on the sidewalk, which stretched across the entire length of the bridge. When we finally reached the other side, we were met by an ECOMOG checkpoint. It was heavily guarded by soldiers wearing full tactical gear including helmets and flak jackets. A half a dozen tanks stood stationary with their barrels already aimed towards the other side of the bridge. Soldiers sat poised behind Browning .50 caliber machine guns anchored on sand bags. The weapon's massive bullets were on a belt waiting to be fed into the gun's chamber. It was a sight to see! We were searched at random and allowed to pass.

We walked up a long staircase passing by several houses before reaching the top of the hill. When I looked back, I had a perfect view of the Johnson Street Bridge. We were at the home of a family friend. When we got inside, the place was already packed with people, who like us, fled from various parts of the country. Ma and pa were given a room and the rest of us slept in the main living area with the other guests. Our host also owned a general store near the bridge so within a few days Curtis and I were put to work.

Living in Monrovia presented its own set of problems. Not only did the rebels continue to attack, but with the influx of thousands of refugees, food and water were scarce. The nearest well was about five miles away from where we stayed. The well owner charged one Liberian dollar (LRD) for every container of water under five gallons and two dollars for larger containers. I was amongst a group of twenty boys from the house who were responsible for transporting water. I made so many trips carrying water on my head that my hair thinned at the top.

Due to the sheer number of people, the well routinely ran low. Eventually, the owner shortened the operating hours to give it time to replenish. This led to lines being formed hours before the well's opening with many leaving their containers as place holders to save their spots. Even with reduced hours, the demand still outran the supply. Often times we purchased muddy water and filtered it through sand bags. The process took several passes and was by no means perfect but it did help to remove most of the dirt.

As for food, we never had enough to eat. Most days consisted of one meal of shared rice. Without our parent's knowledge, we boys hustled for additional food by begging, trading and even stealing. We then snuck out of the house in the middle of the night, went into the nearby woods and held a secret cookout that we called the "Midnight Boo-tee". Sometimes we gathered as much as three times a week cooking rice, fish or whatever else we managed to get our hands on. Because curfew was still in effect, we cooked inside of a steel drum in order to conceal the fire. One night, we had just finished cooking when an ECOMOG soldier stumbled upon us. As soon as we saw him, we took off running! He yelled that it was OK for us to continue. We were relieved and despite the close call, we were not deterred from having future gatherings.

In early November 1992, the rebels continued to hammer Monrovia. Soon they were at the other end of the Johnson Street Bridge. Ironically enough, the house was so close that we could literally see the fighting from the window. The ECOMOG soldiers were armed with heavy weaponry and doing everything they could to keep the rebels from crossing the bridge.

One evening, the rebels launched a massive bombardment campaign on the city. The explosions were non-stop as RPG's and mortar shells crashed onto the capital. We kept watch outdoors all night for fear that a rocket would land on the house. I was a nervous wreck and felt like I would poop in my pants.

By the early morning, we were all exhausted but the fighting raged on. From what I could tell, the ECOMOG troops were outnumbered. I thought that it would only be a matter of time before the rebels stormed the city and God only knew what would happen next. Suddenly, a strange humming sound came from the sky. It was like nothing that I had heard before. Two F4 Phantom Fighter jets emerged overhead following one another. They flew up into the air and then did a nose dive dropping missiles one after the other. Each missile ripped through the sky leaving behind a trail of smoke. They hit just beyond the bridge and the explosive impact roared like rolling thunder. The orange flames flashed brightly and devoured everything within its reach. And just like that, the shooting ceased and the jets took off. On the ground everything went quiet. My jaw dropped trying to comprehend what had just happened. Over the next few days, things seemed to settle down so my brothers and I went back to working at the general store. We stocked shelves. The store carried packaged foods, medicine, household and beauty supplies. There was also a small section near the front door where patrons sat down and ordered alcohol. Since the checkpoint was just outside, the ECOMOG soldiers were our best customers. They loved Club Beer, locally brewed and bottled in Monrovia. We also had a small selection of liquor like rum, gin and cane juice, a local version of moonshine distilled from sugar cane.

My first experience with alcohol came about while working at the general store. An ECOMOG soldier asked if I drank before and I answered no. He joked that I was not a man and slid me a shot of rum. I looked at the owner and he told me to go ahead. I quickly picked up the glass and chugged the brown liquid down. It immediately burned my throat like acid. I let out a howling screech followed by deep breaths in and out hoping for some relief. Everyone in the store laughed. I could not believe that they willingly consumed this poison. As I tried to pull myself together, the soldier patted me on the chest announcing my proclamation of manhood. He could have kept it! I vowed never to drink again.

One afternoon, gunfire rang out. We took cover inside the store like a bunch of school kids participating in an emergency drill. We had become so conditioned to lying on our bellies, that it was an automatic reaction. It became a running joke that the sound of bullets was music to our ears. The tempo was fast paced with a mix of snare and bass drums. It was as if two drum lines were going head to head. After some time, I got up the nerve to peek out the front door. I saw ECOMOG soldiers positioned fifty yards away shooting into the swamp. Luckily, not only did the returning rebel RPG fire miss us, but within a few minutes an ECOMOG air strike was called in. The jet made three quick passes lighting up everything in the swamp. **SILENCE.**

In the months to follow, the fighting sounds grew more and more distant until they eventually ceased. Pa decided that Curtis and I would go with him to check on our house. It took a while but eventually we found a driver who was willing to take us part of the way. As we walked along the road for the last leg of our trip, the aftermath of the intense fighting became more visible. Most of the houses were burnt down. My heart sank as I envisioned what we were about to discover. Fortunately, our house and most of those around it, were still intact. With the exception of some Nigerian soldiers nearby, the neighborhood was empty. The soldiers advised that we should not return to our house because there were rebel splinter cells nearby and fighting could erupt at any moment. We gathered a few items and decided to head back to Monrovia. Little did I know, this would be the last time that I would ever lay eyes on the home that I had always known.

As we were leaving, pa ran into a neighbor who was also returning to check on his house. All of a sudden, the two ECOMOG soldiers standing not too far ahead of us pulled their rifles and started shooting between two houses. Just beyond them, we saw a group of rebels returning fire. We all took off running in the opposite direction. The bullets whisked past my ear like a bee in supersonic flight. With all of the close calls since the war began, this day I was certain that death would find me. Her bite would be painful but quick. My body would find its final resting place in Morris' Farm, the place that I called home.

I came back to reality to find pa not too far ahead of me. He looked like a cartoon character doing a combination of ducking, running and hopping. I'm not sure if he thought his technique would help avoid the bullets but it was actually comical. When we finally made it out of the hot zone, we all chuckled about it. We continued to walk for another two miles before we could find someone willing to drive us back to the city. As we drove, I came to the realization that our every move was being dictated by someone other than ourselves. We were captives. But...this was war, an ever-lurking beast, sometimes chasing, other times patiently waiting but always present. I just longed to be free.

11 VAGABOND

We were constantly moving, never having a permanent place to call home.

By the end of December, the ECOMOG soldiers continued to hammer the rebels. They were joined by the United Liberation Movement of Liberia for Democracy (ULIMO), a group that also fought alongside the Sierra Leonean army against the Revolutionary United Front (RUF). Collectively, the ECOMOG and ULIMO pushed the rebels back towards Kakata. During that time, we ended up moving back to our drugstore in Gardnersville. Fortunately, it was still intact.

Curtis and I helped to run the store since the former employee never returned. It was nice to be a part of the family business. During the day, while ma was at work, people trickled in and out but most of the traffic came in the evenings. Our top seller was Valium 10 milligram tablets, which sold two for five Liberian dollars (LRD). It was purchased mostly by civilians and police officers. Some popped it right into their mouths immediately after buying it. We told them not to take it with alcohol, but most of them walked out of our store and headed straight into the bar next door. We later found out that alcohol was not the house special being served but rather marijuana which was grown right outside of the bar's back door. The five finger plants were fully encaged. I saw the owner pick the leaves and dry them on top of his roof. He would watch over his cash cow like a hawk. As for me, I never really understood addiction. I mean, I knew that marijuana was a drug that should not be used but I never blinked an eye at selling pills. It was a common practice and I figured if someone asked for a certain medication, it was because they legitimately needed it. No prescriptions were required.

By September 1993, pa heard about a resettlement program in Sierra Leone that assisted refugees with placement in America. To think that there was a possibility that I could go there was mind-blowing! "America, the land of milk and honey," the elders would say! I had long dreamt about living in the place that was free of suffering and where everyone was rich. A friend of mine had relatives who were lucky enough to live there. Once, they came to visit and the entire community gathered around just to get a glimpse of the royal family. Everyone went out of their way to touch their fancy clothes and smell their sweet fragrance. Those who had not seen them in a while commented about their light complexions and noticeable weight gain. They would say, "Ayyyy...bright woman. You too fine-oh!" or "Look at him, he looking too fat-oh!" It was all complimentary. Being fat was an indicator of good health and wealth.

Those same relatives sent my friend a VCR and VHS tapes with all kinds of American programming and music videos. I thought that the VCR was the coolest thing! I wished that we could afford one. I sat in awe when we watched Lionel Ritchie's video for "All Night Long". People of all races danced together in the cleanest streets that I had ever seen. Everyone was dressed in nice, vibrantly colored clothes that were obviously not hand-me-downs. The girls were so beautiful with long, flowing hair and most of all, everyone looked happy. There was no way that they were experiencing anything remotely close to what we were going through.

Even with all of the excitement about the possibility of going to America, I was very reluctant to return to Sierra Leone. All I could think about was the conditions that we left under the last time. There was no way that I wanted to be back in a war zone. The word was that the Sierra Leonean army had the upper hand against the RUF, but you just never knew. Pa still made the decision that the two of us would go to find out more information about the resettlement program. We caught a cab six miles to West Point, one of the worst slums in Liberia. It was waste infested and overcrowded with tin shacks. As we approached the transportation area, the stench was unbearable. We boarded a reconfigured cargo van with twenty other people. The van was outfitted with wooden benches, open side panels and a raised cage top for storage. It was so jammed pack that people hung off the back causing it to slump low to the ground.

The ninety-mile trip to the town of Bo Waterside, in Grand Cape Mount County, took all day. By the time we reached the border, it was dark. Pa was surprised to learn that the Mano River Bridge, which connected Liberia and Sierra Leone, was closed down. The driver dropped us off at a nearby village, Bombomhun, and advised that we could cross the border via canoe in the morning. As people unloaded their cargo and quickly disappeared, it was clear that they were not strangers to the area. I looked at pa, shrugged and walked over to the side of a nearby hut.

There, I laid on the ground using my bag as a pillow. I settled into the darkness quickly feeling the ground's moisture seep through my clothes. Through the starlight, I saw pa's silhouette slowly making its way over. He stood looking around.

"Ya'll alright?" a voice said. The figure shined a flashlight on us and then back at himself. It was an armed ULIMO soldier. "Ya'll just come with da last car?"

"Yes," pa responded.

"Don't stay out here. Come to my place."

We followed him into his hut, which was already dimly lit, by a lantern. He showed us over to the bed and asked if we needed anything before he left. Pa declined and we immediately turned in for the night.

I woke up bright and early the next morning while pa was still asleep. Sunlight peeked through a small makeshift window covered with sticks weaved together like a checkerboard. As I sat on the edge of the straw bed looking around, I noticed that the small space only had two other items that I could see. There was an old metal trunk and an AK-74 assault rifle propped up against the wall next to the bed. I eased off the bed trying not to disturb pa. As usual, he snored like a grizzly bear.

I had never held a gun before so I anxiously picked it up. A part of me was intrigued that the gun had the power to instill so much fear and take lives. Clenching my jaws, I closed one eye and focused on the iron sight on top of the gun's barrel. I aimed it at the wall imagining myself pulling the trigger. I had no specific target, I just wanted to know what it felt like. It was actually lighter than what I thought it would be. For a split second, I imagined myself as a child soldier. I don't know why. Maybe because they looked like me or perhaps I had seen them carrying this type of gun. I'm not sure. All of a sudden, there was a double tap on the wooden door.

"Da key-new coming!"

I was so startled that I dropped the gun just as pa woke up. Luckily, he did not notice or worst yet, it did not go off. We gathered our bags and headed to the river.

Because it was the rainy season, the water was moving extremely fast. It sounded like a stampede of Class V rapids. We walked about a half mile up river to catch the canoe so that the current did not cause us to pass our destination while crossing. Before boarding, pa paid the man on the shore. We climbed inside the antiquated vessel with four other passengers and three operators, all of whom appeared to be in their early twenties. Outfitted with flip flops and sleeveless t-shirts, the men strategically placed themselves in the front, middle and rear of the canoe. As soon as I noticed that the middle operator was holding a bucket, my nerves shot up! *Why would someone be assigned such a duty?* Not that it would have mattered under the conditions, but I could not swim. I kept imagining myself being engulfed by the monstrous river.

As soon as we pushed off, the operators broke out in song. They were like seasoned warriors heading into battle. "*Mo-ney, mo-ney, mooo-ney...FIRE COAL! Every-body shake your bod-y ...FIRE COAL!*" Immediately, water began to shoot into the canoe at every angle. It was at that moment that I noticed all the holes and failed patches. The middle man stayed in constant movement scraping the plastic bucket against the wooden floor then tossing the water overboard. The chiseled tail and front operators worked in tandem paddling vigorously against the raging river. All the while, the chant continued, "*Mo-ney, mo-ney, mooo-ney...FIRE COAL! Every-body shake your bod-y...FIRE COAL!*" I held on for dear life as the river tossed us about. Eventually, we made it across safely and I was relieved.

We were let off at a small village and immediately met by Sierra Leonean soldiers who asked why we were entering the country. Pa told them that we were from there and just returning home from Liberia. They explained that there was no transportation in the area due to recent RUF attacks. Any travel would need to be by foot and at our own risk. Pa thanked them and as with other checkpoints, gave them money before we continued on our eighty-mile journey towards Kenema.

We traveled primarily on dirt roads without a single person or vehicle in sight. It was so hot and muggy that I was relieved each time we stumbled across a small stream. "Drink up," pa would say. He would make cups out of big leaves. We would drink and he would say, "Let's keep moving." No matter the circumstances, pa always remained the same. Mr. Even-Keeled. We mostly walked in silence to the patter of our feet and the cries of monkeys, birds and whatever else lurked in the dense jungle. Honestly, the animals were the least of my worries. Having an encounter with the RUF would have been way more dangerous.

After walking several hours, we were drenched with sweat when we reached the village of Malema, located in the southern province of the country. Malema was guarded by six Sierra Leonean soldiers. Once I saw their faces light up, I knew that they had not seen many travelers and that we were in for it. They started by searching our bags and asking our reason for traveling as we had grown accustomed to at other checkpoints. Shortly thereafter, the harassment started.

"So...what do you have for us?" one of the soldiers asked pa in Krio. Pa dug into his pocket and with a closed fist released the balled up bills into the hand of the commander. "What is dis?" he said, looking at the bills with disgust. "Dis is not enough!"

As pa reached into his other pocket, the commander turned to the soldiers with a smirk as if he had just woken up on Christmas morning. Pa handed him more money.

"What else you got?"

"Dat's it," pa said matter-of-factly.

I knew he was lying. Pa always placed his stash in his underwear, strategically leaving what he wanted to spare in his pocket. It made me nervous thinking about what might happen if someone discovered his trickery. It was all really disgusting in my opinion. We paid the rebels, we paid the government troops...no one could be trusted!

As we stood there, the soldiers continued rummaging through our bags. When they divided up my *Warlord* comic books, I was crushed. Each story detailed World War II spy adventures in modern language. I loved that series but I too stole it from the school library so easy come, easy go.

By midnight, we were only halfway there so pa decided that we would hike up the mountain to my grandma's village to sleep for the evening. Luckily for us, the incline of this particular trail was not as grueling as the one we used on our prior trip. Too bad we could not say the same for the humidity. Our wet bodies were definitely an attraction for the pesky mosquitos. They were relentless in their pursuit! Eventually, we reached the top. Most of the villagers were asleep so we quietly made our way to grandma's hut. After some quick conversation and a meal, we turned in for the night.

At first light, we headed back down the mountain and found a mid-sized village that had transportation to Kenema. Pa explained that we were going to stay at his cousin's house. I could not help but wonder just how many relatives he had. While I knew that some of the people that we encountered were his blood relatives, a lot of them were not. What I learned from pa over the years was that he had a very strong affinity to his village. Anyone with ties there was considered family and held in high regard. There were a lot of times growing up when we accommodated visitors from his village at our house. He would introduce them as his brother or sister when in actuality he only had two blood brothers and one blood sister. He would go over and above for them and I used to get so annoyed wishing that he demonstrated that same passion for us day to day. Anyway, it was something that I got used to.

As we traveled along the dirt road, I stared out into the jungle. I drifted off into my thoughts of America. I wanted to sink my teeth into the juicy cheeseburger that I always believed was a staple in American culture. Really, all of the food depicted in the movies looked delicious! As we approached a village, there was a checkpoint. We were all asked to step out of the van so that it could be searched. While waiting, I overheard a soldier asking the driver if he had anything for him. Trying to appease the boss man, the driver overly sold his excitement in honoring the bribe. He smiled and nodded repeatedly as he emptied out his pockets seemingly handing over all that he had. He would do this same "shuck and jive" at the next few checkpoints on our journey. I was just happy that we did not encounter any fighting before finally arriving in Kenema.

Pa's cousin's house was on a single level with five bedrooms. There were multiple families living there and to my surprise I saw an old acquaintance. It was Isata, one of the girls that used to bring me my meals in the village. She was still infatuated with me! In fact, I caught her pointing and giggling with the other girls. I can't say that I minded the attention. If anything, it raised my stock a bit!

After a few days in Kenema, pa said that he needed to go and take care of some business. It ended up being two months before he returned. I had become comfortable with my surroundings so I really didn't mind. I spent most of my time hanging out with Isata. We actually became good friends. It broke my heart when she dropped the bomb that she would soon be marrying a forty something year old man from the village. The dowry had already been paid and it was just a matter of time. She seemed so nonchalant about it. I mean, it was clear that she liked me, but yet and still she was already purchased. I was curious, for more reasons than one, as to whether or not she was still a virgin. She explained that she was and that her father would kill her if it was found that she had sex before her wedding day. In fact, as she explained, it was customary to display a bloodied sheet as proof of virginity the morning after consummation.

One day, I accompanied Isata to wash clothes in the river. As we were talking, a group of boys from the house approached us.

"*Lek ooman! Lek ooman!*" Salieu jeered. Unsurprisingly, the other boys joined in. He always had control over the pack. They ran together in everything that they did so other than a passing *kushe* or hello, I really just hung out with the girls. So it was no surprise to hear them refer to me as being like a woman, not that I liked it any. I shot a look and Salieu immediately piped down his minions. He told me to come with them fishing. *How did he know?* I had not partook in my favorite pastime since leaving Gardnersville so I was chomping at the bit – no pun intended.

By the time I could say *tata o*r goodbye to Isata, the pack had already taken off into the jungle. I darted behind them trying to catch up. Their bare backs shifted quickly left, right, down, leaping up and over the elements. They were like seasoned, slipper-clad warriors navigating through the thick bush with ease. I, on the other hand, was a frail boy trying my best to save face and keep up. I thought to myself, *maybe I am the city boy that my uncle claimed me to be.* I mean, I had spent a large portion of my life venturing on jungle trails with my brothers but traveling with the pack was different. They were fearless and unfazed by anything. Yet, the slice of the razor sharp leaves, mixed with the sweat of my brow, took its toll on me.

"Stop!" Salieu yelled to the pack. They complied

immediately, waiting as I made my way towards them obviously struggling. With a smirk on his face he said, "Lamin, turn round!"

The others laughed adding that I had not seen anything yet. For a brief moment, I contemplated taking the out but I knew that this meant losing their respect and suffering whatever backlash would come my way until pa returned. Not to mention, it would probably be easier to push on with the group than getting lost trying to backtrack on my own.

"No!" I pushed back, trying to catch my breath. I wanted to show them that I was up for the challenge. As my thoughts settled, I heard a familiar sound. It was water and it was nearby. We continued walking and soon came to a clearing. Upon stepping out, we were only a few feet from a cliff's edge. It overlooked a river gorge some twenty feet down. I was so relieved that we had reached the end of our journey. I asked Salieu if they brought enough string to reach the river. He smiled and pointed over to the right. It was a tree that had fallen from the other side of the river bank and landed not too far from where we stood. Its top was so massive that it blended into the rest of the brush so I did not even notice it. *No way,* I thought! This river is clearly impassable. I was petrified and tried my best not to let it show. The log was only about a foot wide, what if I slipped or misjudged my step? As I stood there trying to grasp the colossal task that stood before me, the pack carried on. Each boy zipped across quickly like an extreme athlete. Oh how I wished that I had crossed already. Now all eyes were on me.

"Lamin, *kam!*" they yelled from the other side telling me to come. I reluctantly maneuvered around some of the branches and placed one foot out and stomped the bark trying to test the stability of the death bridge. "*Kam!*" the voices impatiently yelled again.

I took a deep breath, placed my flip flops on my wrists, extended my arms straight out to each side and stepped my bare feet out onto the tree trunk. My heart raced with each slow and carefully placed step. Realizing that the pack's foot over foot approach was not going to work for me, I slowly turned my lower body sideways and opted instead for a slide and drag technique. I carefully slid my front foot and then drug my back foot to meet it. In my head, the more my feet maintained contact with the wood, the safer I would be. I tried to stabilize myself with all that I had, curling my toes like eagle talons over the rugged wood. *Don't look down,* I thought. *Focus on the wood ahead. Wait a minute, that part looks rotted.* My heart rate sped back up and I could hardly catch my breath. *It's too late to turn back now,* I thought, *you're in the middle of this death trap.* My body froze as I glanced over at the pack. Their mouths were moving but I could no longer hear them. Time stood still and the only sounds were the water beneath me and my heart's thump. *Shit! Now what?* Beads of sweat stung my eyes but I was too afraid of losing my balance to reach up and wipe it.

"*Ep mi!*", I yelled to the pack. Obviously impressing the group was no longer relevant. No one could help me. They motioned for me to keep moving but I couldn't because my legs felt like they were going to give out at any moment. *Think, BK, think!* Slowly, I eased down and straddled the log between my clenched thighs. I carefully scooched along until I reached the other side of the river. By the time I made it, the boys were laughing hysterically. They called me every cowardly name that they could think of. I gladly accepted the titles and even laughed at myself.

The next order of business was to cut some bamboo and construct rods using the string and hooks that Salieu brought. We then walked down the bank to the river and dug up worms for bait. Little did they know, I was a fishing expert. I caught catfish left and right and ended up with the most catches that day. The pack was impressed, almost to the point where they forgot about the tree incident. Well...that was until we made our return trip! The fishing excursion was the beginning of a friendship with the boys. We only got to hang out for a few more weeks before pa returned. On the way out, it was the same old routine, thanks and well wishes. For as bad as it sounds, I was happy that there were no lasting bonds established. It just made the goodbyes that much easier. Unfortunately, this was the harsh reality of war. We were constantly moving, never having a permanent place to call home.

Pa and I caught a bus into Freetown and walked about two miles to his cousin's place. It was a huge six-bedroom house built into the slope of a mountain. The panoramic view, from what appeared to be a floating deck, was absolutely breathtaking! There was an endless array of lush green trees that filtered through just the right amount of sunlight every morning and seemingly embraced the sunset each evening. To the left of the house was a stream that could be seen and heard flowing down the mountain. It was so tranquil that I often found myself reminiscing about my favorite spot on the side of my house in Paynesville. The shade from the Yellow Wood tree gave me many days of relief from the scorch of the sun. I listened to the melodic sounds of the birds that sat perched on its branches. The smell of cassava leaf soup filled the air as ma was always cooking. Sometimes my brothers and I played the Ludo board game or debated about who was the best at something with the winner getting the loser's share of rice. Oh, how I wished that I could live in those moments once more.

Over the course of the next month, I got to know those in the house while pa spent most days heading into town to inquire about the resettlement program. As a newcomer, everyone took interest in me asking a lot of questions about Liberian culture. One of the most common questions was about how I spoke. They wanted to know why my English was so broken. To eliminate confusion, I spoke Krio as often as possible. Most evenings we went to the stream to get water and wash clothes. Other locals were there doing the same with some openly bathing. Nudity was an accepted practice so I tried my best not to stare or get aroused for that matter. I took everything in stride figuring that this would be yet another story to tell my brothers.

Eventually, pa realized that things were not progressing as planned with the resettlement program so he decided that we should return to Liberia. We went to Kenema to find transportation but learned that trips to the Liberian border had ceased because the Sierra Leonean war was escalating. The word on the street was that for the right amount of money the military would allow civilians to ride in their trucks. Pa found out the departure times and within a few days we were set to go or so I thought.

Upon arriving to the transportation area, pa disclosed that I would be making the journey to Liberia alone. This would give him time to focus more diligently on trying to get us to America. I accepted the task as just another thing that I needed to do. Not to mention, I was going to be under military escort so I felt safe. Before boarding, pa gave me a big loaf of bread and one thousand Liberian dollars (LRD) which he anticipated would cover the additional transportation costs throughout the trip. He warned me to keep the money hidden until I needed it and to eat the bread sparingly. Then, he approached one of the adult travelers and asked him to keep an eye on me. We bid farewell and I climbed up onto one of the truck's huge tires and pulled myself into the bed. There were six Sierra Leonean soldiers clad in battle uniforms and ten other civilians, mostly women, on board. All were older than me. The soldiers were generally jovial, focusing most of their attention on the female passengers. I laughed to myself at some of their pickup lines. Even I knew better than to tell a girl that her body was "fine". I quickly stepped around them and found a spot in the back on the truck. I could not wait to get *home* to my family!

12 ALONE

I needed my family like never before but all I had was myself.

It was early afternoon when we set out on the slow moving journey filled with unpaved and eroded roads. I knew that the 200-mile trip to Gardnersville was going to take forever. Nevertheless, the turtle's crawl gave me a chance to take in the jungle and villages that we passed along the way. The colorfully dressed villagers and men carrying banana sacks reminded me of my grandma's village. With the exception of the soldiers who stood lookout around the perimeter of the truck bed and me standing in the back, everyone else sat near the front of the truck. I watched as a few of the Liberian women took turns braiding one another's hair. At times, they spoke loudly over the sound of the truck sharing stories back and forth about everything from neighborhood gossip to trading of merchandise. When the conversation was especially juicy, they emphasized their position by sucking their teeth and exclaiming "I beg you *yah!*" Occasionally, they leaned over one another and laughed at their private jokes. Others conversed in their native dialects. After traveling most of the day, we stopped at what appeared to be a military camp. All of the soldiers got off the truck and gathered before one of the commanders. I leaned over the rail slightly and overheard them discussing numerous attacks in the area ahead. *Here we go again,* I thought, hoping that the report was wrong. After chatting a bit, they gathered ammunition and we were back on the road. I retook my position staring out the rear of the truck. This time I was more focused on spotting rebels lurking in the bush. Not that I could have done anything about it, but somehow I felt like I was doing my part. The truck continued to wobble about on the road. We ducked down at times to avoid the overhanging branches from the nearby trees. We had not passed a single vehicle. It was a good thing because the dirt road was barely wide enough to hold the massive truck. The roaring of the engine echoed throughout the forest each time the driver shifted gears.

All of a sudden, we came up on a smoldered Red Cross SUV that was flipped onto its side. I could not believe it! The Red Cross had helped so many of us with food and medicine since the war begun. I saw them traveling, seemingly without incident, behind rebel lines in Kakata. *What would make someone attack them? Was there a rebel ambush?*

Without warning, the soldiers opened fire with a rash of automatic weaponry. The truck sped up and rocked all over the road making it difficult for everyone to maintain balance. I hovered down on the bed of the truck as hot bullet shells stung my head. The smell of gunpowder choked me and the smoke that engulfed the air robbed me of my sight. I could not help but think that a RPG would be coming. How quickly the scene turned into déjà vu of

Liberia. I needed my family like never before but all I had was myself.

ROARRRRRRR! The driver desperately tried to maintain control of the five-ton steel wagon, which was obviously being pushed to its limits. *ROARRRRRRR!*

"Stop! Stop!" one of the soldiers yelled and the shooting stopped. The men remained poised with their weapons pointed into the jungle as the truck gradually reduced speed. Trying to regain my balance, I slowly stood to my feet. All of the passengers were visibly shaken by the whole ordeal. The soldier advised that we did not take any return fire. I was glad that their offensive tactics paid off.

It was dark by the time we made it to a village along the border. This was the same place that I recall passing through with pa when we got off the deadly canoe ride. It certainly looked different in the black of night. The village was very quiet as most of the people were indoors. There were, however, soldiers standing guard. All of the women from our group were led into a building to sleep. Myself and the other lone civilian male were taken to an unfinished building and told that we could sleep there. It was so dark inside that I could not make out my surroundings. A glimpse of light flickered from an outside fire that the soldiers sat around. I was so mentally and physically tired that I made my way to what felt like a clear spot and lowered down onto the ground to go to sleep. Just then, my stomach growled and I remembered that pa sent me with a loaf of bread. As I was about to eat the bread, I felt compelled to share it with the group. I gave some to the man and then made my way back to the women giving each person a small piece. I ate my share before falling asleep.

Within a few hours, I was awakened by the chill of night, which easily made its way through the open holes in the walls where the windows would eventually be. I called out to the man and asked if he was awake. He responded yes and suggested that we huddle together. We did just that and it warmed us up a little bit. We spent the night going in and out of sleep and talking about the day's events. At daybreak, I caught first glimpse of our sleeping quarters. It was essentially barren ground within an unfinished house. There were old buckets of muddy water and other tools left behind by the builders of the house. We walked back to where the soldiers dropped us off the night before. A lot of the villagers were up. Some cooked food on the open fire. It smelled amazing! While I was tempted to buy something, I remembered that the money that I was given had to last the entire trip. As such, I sat and waited for instructions for our next leg.

The soldiers escorted the six of us who needed to cross into Liberia down to the river. One of the female passengers inquired about the cost of the canoe ride and subsequent transport from the Liberian border to Monrovia. I immediately realized that I did not have enough money to cover the cost of the entire trip. I stood there trying to figure out what I was going to do.

"You alright?" one of the women asked. Her eyes flashed a look of concern.

"I not got enough money-oh," I replied.

"I didn't forget what you done for us last night." She smiled placing her hand on my shoulder. "Dere was no food and you gave us some of your bread." With a quick wink, she walked over and paid the operator for both of our fares. I was so relieved. I expressed my sincere gratitude as we boarded the canoe.

On the other side of the river, there was a pickup truck waiting. It was already filled with other passengers and a load of charcoal so only four people from our group were able to fit. Myself and the man from the sleeping quarters volunteered to stay behind. The driver said that there may be another truck coming through later that day.

As we waited in the village, I took a look around. I saw

the villagers going about their daily routines while armed ULIMO soldiers manned the area. I had not eaten so I was ecstatic to see fruit trees. I ate all that I could and by early afternoon another truck came. We jumped in with other villagers and headed to Monrovia. Since the rainy season just finished, the road conditions were very bad. Erosion left a lot of uneven surfaces and deep potholes. At times, the vehicle's tires fell into foot deep craters causing the truck to dip suddenly. All the bouncing back and forth gave me motion sickness so without warning I hurled out the window. On occasion, I was able to yell for the driver to stop so that I could dart out just in the nick of time. I was so embarrassed.

After a very long day, we arrived at a local village. It was evening and I was glad to find out that the driver prearranged our stay at a house. We even received a small bowl of rice from our host. I was still a little nauseous from the trip but my hunger took precedence. After we ate, we all slept in the living room. The indoor concrete floor was a welcomed upgrade from my prior night.

The next morning, we rose early and headed back out on the road. A few hours into the trip, I felt sick again. The other passengers were visibly annoyed that I was prolonging our travel. Eventually, we reached the paved highway. From there, it was a straight shot into Monrovia with the exception of a few checkpoints. We were dropped off at the busy transportation hub of Freeport. Ironically, it was the same place where my family and I docked when we first returned to Liberia. I was happy to be home. I parted ways with the other travelers and caught a taxi with the remaining money that I had left. It was twilight when the driver dropped me off in Gardnersville, down the street from our drugstore. After three days of traveling, my clothing was covered with red dust and my hair was matted to my head. As I started up the road, I noticed ma standing in front of the store leaning on the rail. I could see her squinting trying to make out who was coming. As I got closer, she recognized me and took off running. She hugged me and praised God that I was alive. It had been some four months since she had last seen me.

"Where ya pa?"

"Da pa-paye stay in Kenema. He sent me by myself."

"Ayyyyy, man! Why Lamin send my baby like dat!" She was visibly upset, sucking her teeth and mumbling to herself. I assured her that I was fine. I figured that the fewer details that I gave her about the three-day journey, the better off pa would be. Unfortunately, there was no way of letting him know that I had made it. For now, we went inside and I enjoyed the luxury of being able to bathe.

13 THE AUDITION

Why would America want us? We were visibly poor and had nothing to offer.

Aside from recovering from my long journey, I spent the next few weeks helping ma and my brothers run the store. I was happy to be back with my family even if it meant that we lived cramped inside of the drugstore. Even the youngest, Beindu and Peter, were doing their part to chip in. As far as my other siblings, ma said that they were all doing well.

The ECOMOG soldiers still patrolled the area, which unfortunately looked no different from when I left. The destruction was massive making it difficult to feel at peace. As much as I attempted to do normal things, like going fishing or considering returning back to school, I never felt comfortable. Everything was so on-again, off-again that I wondered what's the use.

By April 1994, pa had been gone for over six months.

We were relieved when he finally showed up. He told us that the resettlement program was about to start and in order to qualify we had to be refugees. This meant going to live at a refugee camp in Sierra Leone. Rather than taking the risk of moving everyone at the same time, just Beindu and I accompanied him. That way if the program failed, we had a place to return to. The very next day, we traveled to take our passport photos and had them in hand by early May.

With a few bags packed, we headed to the Spriggs Payne Airport located eleven miles from the drugstore. I had passed the small, single-story building several times in the past while heading to the Sinkor marketplace. I never imagined that I would actually be flying. Inside the terminal, there was not too much to see. Pa already had the tickets so we just sat down and waited until they announced that it was time to board.

We walked outside onto a paved air strip to meet our plane. I was excited and extremely nervous about my first flight. We walked up the steps and before boarding were met by an airline worker who scanned our bodies with a handheld metal detector. Pa and Beindu sat next to one another and I sat across the aisle. Once the engine started, my nerves shot up! For the life I me, I could not keep still. I felt sorry for the passenger sitting next to me because he had already settled in and seemed to be dozing off. After receiving instructions from the flight attendant, I fastened my seat belt. The next thing I knew, we were moving. We went faster and faster and faster! My body was pinned to the seat. It was awesome! All of a sudden, we lifted up off of the ground. I couldn't believe it! I peeked around the man to get a better view from the window. The coastline and the beauty of the ocean was amazing! As we climbed, the plane shook so I immediately sat back in my seat. He sensed my tension and told me not to worry, that it was just "bumpy air". *Bumpy air?* I was so relieved when it passed. The higher we went up, the more Monrovia looked like a scaled architectural model. A true work of art. Beindu said something to me and I could hardly hear her because my ears were clogged. They eventually popped just like they had when we climbed up the mountain to grandma's village.

We landed at Hastings Airport near Freetown fairly quickly... well at least in comparison to how we were used to traveling. From there we caught a taxi eight miles to the town of Waterloo and walked on forest trails to the refugee camp. By the time we made it, we were exhausted. People stared as we walked by as if they knew we were strangers. I was pleasantly surprised at how good the camp looked. I expected tents but instead there were hundreds of small huts built alongside an old air strip. The area was surrounded by oil palm trees backed by a huge forest.

Pa already reconnected with our relatives from Grand Bassa County who lived with us during the onset of the war. I was excited that we would be staying with them at the camp. In total, there were seven of them already living in a hut made with interwoven sticks and mud. The roof was constructed from palm leaves. As we settled in the first night, I thought *please don't let me knock over the burning candles* because everything, including our beds made from hay bales, would have quickly engulfed in flames!

It did not take long to see that the area was cramped. Since there was no outside assistance, the battle for food and water was ongoing. This was nothing new for me. Most days we ate white rice with palm oil. A single well sat on the far side of the camp operated by a hand cranked pump. Although there was a limit of one container per visit, the line was always long. I made it a priority to find other means. Living in my grandma's village taught me that there were many sources of water in the jungle. One day, while out on the trails, I saw a hole in the ground with water coming out of it. It tasted good so that became my secret place to go whenever pa sent me for water.

After a few weeks, my older brother Francis came to live with us in hopes that he too would get accepted into the resettlement program. I was so excited to see him since he had not lived at home for some time. He did, however, come by on occasion. Usually he was driving some fancy car of a big shot government official that he chauffeured for. He would take me out and show me off to all of his friends. He was a real ladies man. In fact, he taught me some of my best moves like the double eyebrow raise and the infamous wink. Man, how I missed my brother!

I took pride in bringing Francis up to speed on the day to day life at the camp. Like me, he was an experienced fisherman. He said that we should build traps to increase efficiency. We sliced bamboo into thin pieces, weaved and tied them together to form three baskets. Next, we crushed seeds from the oil palm trees and put them inside the traps as bait. Then, the traps were attached to strings with sticks on the opposite ends anchored into the bank. They were tossed into the water and left overnight.

When we would return the next morning, we would find catfish, turtles, blue crabs and crawfish. People at the camp started asking where we went to make our catch. Figuring that they might steal our traps or take over our spot, we never told them. The fishing was so effortless that we decided to build and set traps in the forest as well. We caught iguanas, possums and porcupines, all of which we had caught before at our farm. The meat was very lean. I especially liked playing with the porcupine spikes. I threw them at Francis like darts and he would get so mad at me!

Francis was more of a natural bushman than I was. He taught me how to retrace my steps through the forest. It involved breaking branches at turns to signal the direction of travel. One day, I ventured into the forest alone to check the traps. While I broke some branches, apparently I did not do it at every turn because I got lost on my way back. Everything looked the same and I did not know what to do. I ran frantically in varying directions hoping to find a quick way out. Nothing worked.

As evening approached, every sound amplified or at least that is how it seemed. Each time I heard a noise, I broke out running as not to have to find out what it was. I was drenched with sweat and could not seem to catch my breath. Just as I thought that all hope was lost, I came across a trail that had obviously been traveled on by others. As I followed it, I heard something in the brush coming at me quickly. This time instead of running, I pulled out my machete. Out of nowhere, Francis popped out. Boy was I relieved! He had been looking for me because it was so close to nightfall. As he lectured me, I just shook my head in agreement never telling him that I got lost.

About a month after arriving at the refugee camp, there was an open call to interview for the resettlement program. Families were given the chance to meet with program staff to learn about the eligibility requirements and to share their reasons for seeking refuge in America. We dressed in our best clothes and caught a bus twenty miles to Freetown. Although it was early in the morning, the line was already wrapped around the building. I spotted several people from the camp including my newfound friend Daddy Boy and his family. They were dressed to kill. I looked down at my oversized dress pants and scuffed up Volt sneakers and quickly concluded that their best was way better than ours. His aunt bragged about how they already had family members in America. We barely stepped foot in the line and I already felt defeated.

As we entered the office, we were invited to take a seat by a Caucasian American woman who sat behind a desk. Pa introduced himself and us. He went on to explain that he worked for VOA and provided her with supporting documentation. The interview was pretty straight forward with questions about our family history and refugee status. While I tried to stay engaged in the conversation, I could not help but to be intrigued by the interviewer. Other than foreign service workers that I saw from afar and actors in videos, I had never been face to face with a white person before. I mean...a real live white person with ghostly complexion, silky fine brown hair and scary blue eyes. I couldn't believe it! I sat there noting our distinct differences and trying not to laugh when she spoke. She really did sound funny speaking that *American Siri* as we called it. American Siri was the accent spoken by American people. There were so many versions of it shown in the movies. For example, in *Beat Street*, the New Yorkers spoke with a yo-yo slang while the cowboys in *The Bad, Good and the Ugly* had a hee-haw twang. Yet and still, in other movies, people spoke a much more proper version of English. All of it sounded strange to me and at times was very hard to understand. It was so bad that I often watched movies for the action and visual effects rather than the dialogue.

A lot of Liberians pretended to acquire American Siri once they had gone to America or had family living there. It was viewed as showing off. So to hear someone make mention that a Liberian was speaking American Siri was not a good thing. My friend, Kema, used to do the best imitation of it. She would say, "Hello. My name is Shelly Barrrrrr-ber" with this proper English accent and her pinky finger pointing out. We would all die with laughter! It was ironic that we wanted to live in America and enjoy all the perks that came with it, but we did not want to lose ourselves. We were and would always be Liberians. There is a certain sense of pride that came with staying true to who we are. No war would ever change that.

With a smirk on my face, I watched as the interviewer directed her questions at my brother.

"How old are you?"

"Twenty-six."

She quickly noted his response and went on asking pa a few additional questions. At the conclusion of the interview, she told us that we should check back in a few weeks. At that time, a list of the names of those moving on to the next round of interviews would be posted. As a side note, she added that Francis was not a qualified dependent because of his age. His face dropped. I could not believe what I was hearing and moreover why was *Shelly Barrrrrr-ber* so casual about it. We walked out of the room in silence. It was sad to think that my brother might not be able to go to America. Then again, I really did not think that any of us stood a chance of going. Why would America want us? We were visibly poor and had nothing to offer. When we got back to the camp, Francis said that he would wait it out until the list came up.

Within a few weeks, the list was posted and it had shrunk substantially. We were so excited to see our names but the feeling quickly faded when we saw the notation next to Francis' name indicating that he was ineligible for a second interview. By the end of the week, he returned back to Liberia. My friend Daddy Boy and his family also learned that they did not make it through to the next round of interviews. I could not believe it! With relatives already living in America and how they looked on the day of the open call, I thought that they were a definite shoo-in. Whatever the reason, we were one step closer towards living in America, so for that, I was thankful.

14 NEW WORLD

A new beginning, a new life and a new walk.

By middle of June 1994, the World Cup started. Football, or soccer as it's referenced in the United States, was almost like a religion. It served as glue for the nation. Football caused people to unite despite their differences and trumped dismal circumstances like war. Liberia never made an appearance in the World Cup, although we boosted arguably one of the best players in the world, George Weah. Nevertheless, everyone rallied in support of all of the African countries that were represented like Cameroon, Morocco and Nigeria. We all gathered around the radio faithfully every day for the play by play coverage. The cheering could be heard all throughout the camp and the "feel-good" camaraderie almost made me forget about the war. It took me back to the day when the Liberian national football team, the Lone Stars, defeated Ghana for

119

the first time. Man, oh man, that was a joyful day!

Over the next month, apart from listening to the football coverage, I spent most of my time fishing. Then, the day finally arrived for our second interview. As I got dressed in the same dress shirt and pants that I wore the first time, I felt compelled to say a little prayer. "God, please help us today in this interview. AMEN." It was short and sweet. Besides, we had to hurry to catch the van.

Since the interview was by appointment, we were the only family there.

"Mr. Brima Lamin?" an older Sierra Leonean woman emerged out of the doorway wearing a black business suit with her hair styled to perfection. My guess was that it was a wig.

"Yes," pa responded.

"Come on in and have a seat." We followed behind her into the small office. I was surprised not to see *Shelly Barrrrrrr-ber*. "I see here that you, your son Brima Kemokai Lamin and your daughter Edna Beindu Lamin have applied for the resettlement program." She peered down into her open folder.

"Yes, dat's correct."

Wait a minute, I thought, *she's not even American. How can she interview us?* I guess it didn't matter as long as she ruled in our favor. I looked up and she was staring directly at me through the two inches of makeup that she had caked on her face. She cracked a grin so I smiled back trying to be polite.

"Your son is very handsome," she said to pa, all the while staring at me.

Eeeeellll! No this old bat is not trying to flirt with me!

"Tanks," pa said.

"Tanks," I reluctantly chimed in, forcing a smile. Hey...if that's what it took!

She smiled again and turned her attention to pa. "Now dat da clearances are complete, da next step will be for you

120

all to have a medical exam, vaccinations and attend an orientation."

Oh my God! Is this really happening! She went on to explain that if the results of the tests were good then we would get our departure date. The program would cover the upfront airfare costs but pa would be responsible for repaying it once we were established in America. We would enter the United States on a refugee status. Once pa received legal residency, he could file for our other family members to come into the country. I could not believe what I was hearing! All my years dreaming about America and now it could finally be a reality! I too could live in a land where war and poverty did not exist. A place where everyone had nice clothes, big houses, cars and plenty of money!

On our way back to the camp, pa warned that other than telling those that we lived with, we should keep our news to ourselves and avoid leaving the immediate area. I honored his request but it was hard to contain my excitement! We followed through with the medical examinations and orientation in Freetown. The orientation was conducted with a few other families. We were given more instructions on pre-departure processing and travel.

By mid-September, pa received a letter at the camp hub advising that we were medically cleared for travel. Since it near our departure date, he said that it was OK to share the news with our closest friends. I had mixed emotions about whether or not to tell Daddy Boy, but I figured that it was better if he heard the news from me. One day, we were hanging out fishing and I just blurted it out.

"We going to America."

"You got accepted?"

"Yes."

"Why you sound so down. Dat's good news."

"I don't know...I guess I just didn't want to hurt you. I mean, I know dat you're happy for me. I jus' wish dat you were going too."

"Yeah, me too." He kept fishing. "When you leave?"

"In about a week."

"Wow! Dat's soon-oh. Does your ma know?"

"Pa sent word, but we don't know if she got it."

"You gon' love America!" I smiled just thinking about it. "Don't forget about me-oh!" He gave me a playful shove.

"You know I won't forget about you."

"I mean it. You better send me something good!"

"I will." We bumped fist and went on fishing.

On the morning of September 25, 1994, pa woke up around 9:00 a.m. I was already dressed in my "interview best" after being up for what seemed like most of the night. My mind was overtaken with thoughts of America and what waited for me there. To know that we were amongst the few families selected, out of the hundreds that applied, felt like nothing short of a miracle.

"BK, you ready?" Pa asked, grabbing a small black bag with his and Beindu's belongings. She was in tow.

"Yeah." I grabbed my knapsack filled with all that I owned...two shirts and two pair of pants. I figured that once we got to America, I probably wouldn't need them. We came outside and there was a large group of our relatives and neighbors gathered nearby. The scene was very awkward and melancholy. It felt more like we walking into a funeral service than a farewell party. Some looked at us with blank stares while others hung their heads low.

"We going-ohhhh!" pa said, making eye contact with our relatives. "Tank you all ever so much."

"Tank you," I chimed in. Just then, I caught a glimpse of Daddy Boy out of the corner of my eye. He was sitting on a cinder block in front of his house staring at the ground. I walked over and squatted down next to him. "Hey."

"Hey." He never looked up.

"I'm gon' miss you," I said, wrapping my arm around his shoulder, gently nudging him. In the midst of his silence, an overwhelming feeling of guilt hit me. I was deserting everyone and everything that I ever loved.

"BK let's go," pa called out.

"Take care Daddy Boy." I stood up and walked away. Our cousin Abraham accompanied us to the pick-up point at the camp hub where we were met by two other families. He waited with us until the van came and said that we would meet again at the ferry. When we arrived in Freetown, we were greeted by a guide and invited to join the other refugees on a bus ride to the ferry. As I looked around at the families, I couldn't help but to miss my own back in Liberia. As far as I knew, they had no idea that we had left the camp. The thought that I might never see them again killed me inside.

After a short ride, we were dropped off at the Kissy Ferry Terminal. People swarmed the dock carrying everything from luggage to items they purchased in the market. Our guide handed out ferry tickets to everyone in the group. We followed him through the entrance where cousin Abraham was already waiting for us. Unlike the wooden ferry that we rode in Guinea, this one was huge with multiple levels. We went to the top deck and watched as vehicles and passengers packed onto the vessel. Beindu and I waved at those on the shore as we pulled out. I wished that my brothers were there with me.

As we got moving, the light breeze coming off of the Sierra Leone River cooled my skin. I could not help but overhear a conversation that cousin Abraham was having with pa. He was talking about me. He basically warned pa that he should keep a tight rein on me once we got to America. His belief was that American culture would turn me away from my traditional African upbringing and the Islamic faith. Little did they know, I had abandoned the faith a long time ago. I was just going through the motions to please pa. The truth to matter was that there was a part of me that was tired of living in secret. I wanted to escape the dictatorship. For me, America seemed like an outlet to do just that. I'm not sure how cousin Abraham sensed it, but he was right.

After about an hour, we arrived at the dock in Lungi. Walking off the ferry felt like stepping into the marketplace at Waterside or Freeport in Liberia. There were vendors, transportation providers and people moving about trying to get to wherever. A bus sat waiting, so we boarded with the other families while cousin Abraham grabbed a cab to meet us at the airport. It was nice of him to see us off. As we drove, I couldn't help but to think about my journey along the way. My time in the jungle with my brothers and the pack, my visit to grandma's village, my solo trip with the Sierra Leonean army and more firsts than I could ever count! What a ride! Through it all, I survived.

The bus stopped and we were at Lungi International Airport. It was huge compared to Hastings and Spriggs Payne. Washed in all white, big glass windows seemingly covered the entire building. Our guide led us to another representative who stood outside with a sign that read "Resettlement". Cousin Abraham joined us and as a group we headed into the airport waiting area. It was late in the afternoon and the airport was not too crowded. Most of the travelers there were dressed in traditional African attire. I was impressed by the professional appearance of the uniformed staff and the inside of the airport itself. It was clean and the white decor carried on throughout the place.

During the few hours that we waited, I noticed a pretty teenage girl with one of the other families. I don't know why I didn't notice her before but I made sure to make eye contact with her. She smiled and quickly turned away. I decided that I would wait to make my move later. When the plane arrived, each family group was called. When we heard our name, we quickly said our goodbyes to cousin

Abraham and headed outside to the airstrip. Security scanned each person at the bottom of the stairway. After making clearance, we were allowed to walk up and into the plane.

I scooched past pa and Beindu to claim my seat next to the window. I didn't want to miss anything! I barely listened when the stewardess gave the flight safety instructions. Her French accent was so thick that it was hard to make out what she was saying anyway. Not to mention the fact that she was very pretty. As we were about to take off, she came by and checked our seatbelts. She quickly reached over and tightened mine.

"How long to America?" I asked anxiously. *Man, she smells good.*

She grinned, "We must connect in Brussels first."

"Brussels?"

"Yes, Brussels, Belgium." She continued walking up the aisle to her seat.

What! I had no idea that we needed to stop in another country. Hopefully, we wouldn't be staying their long.

"Cleared for take-off" I heard over the speaker. Take off was smooth and soon we were soaring in the clouds. I spent most of my time looking out the window. Once it got dark, I ate a few snacks and rested. Beindu and pa did the same. As we prepared for landing, the lights from the city lit up the dark sky. It revealed the most beautiful European architecture! Somehow the world had changed in a matter of six hours.

We stepped off the plane and into the jetway leading into the airport. As soon as we came through the gate, there stood a white man with a sign that read "Liberian Resettlement". Our group approached him and he told us to follow him. He too had a heavy French accent. As we walked, I was in awe of the massive facility. I had never seen anything so impressive. It was a far cry from the African airports. People, white people, were everywhere!

Most of them seemed to be in a hurry. Even still, they took time for double and even triple takes of our large group. Some outright stared as if they had never seen black people before. I didn't mind because I was staring at them too. I had never seen so many *Shelly Barrrrrrr-ber's!* Imagining them all with their pinkies pointed out, I giggled to myself and kept on moving.

I was introduced to so many new things in that airport. My head spun at every turn and I could hardly contain my excitement! To see stairs that moved up and down and walkways that carried people effortlessly was astounding! Over the course of my life, I had walked what seemed like millions of miles and now I discovered that people in other parts of the world didn't have to. Irony or fate, I was exposed to possibilities that exceeded all that I could have ever imagined. I couldn't wait to get to America!

When we arrived at the gate, there was a large sign that read "Sabena Airlines". Other passengers already sat waiting so we joined them over near the windows. I tried to catch a glimpse of the action outdoors but instead only got a few flashes of light in the darkness. It had already been a very long day so even the excitement could no longer carry me. I decided to rest using my knapsack as a pillow. Eventually, an announcement was made in both English and French that it was time to board the flight to New York. The guide gathered our group and we were allowed to go onto the aircraft first. The plane was massive with two levels. Each row seated eight people across grouped in three sections with aisles in between. I was glad to have gotten a window seat even though I could not see much through the darkness. I made it my business to visually locate the girl that I made eye contact with back at the airport. She was just a few rows ahead of us. The plane was more than half empty so it did not take long for the entire boarding process to be completed.

After take-off, the stewardess came by and asked if I

wanted chicken or beef tips for dinner. I had never heard of beef tips so I figured that I would try something new. It was only after I started eating that I realized beef tips were just a fancy name for cow meat. Well at least that was what we called it back home. The difference was that I was accustomed to it being tough but this meat melted on my tongue.

Shortly after dinner the lights dimmed, the television monitors flipped down and we watched a movie. A few people walked around so I decided that it was a good time to use the bathroom and scope out the scene. When I was headed back to my seat, I noticed that the girl had conveniently moved away from the adults and now sat in an empty row. I walked up to her and introduced myself. She invited me to sit down and we started talking about where we lived and the war. It was hard to believe that we both lived in the camp but our paths never crossed. She was just as excited as I was about life in America.

The adults came by a few times to check on us but they slept most of plane ride. I was too anxious to sleep and why should I when I had the company of a beautiful girl. The hours passed by so quickly and before we knew it, people started cheering. Apparently, we had ignored all of the announcements because when we ran to the window it was daylight. There were tall buildings everywhere! We were landing at John F. Kennedy International Airport in New York. I thought, *oh my God, I am finally here*. All that I had been through up until this point, led me to this very moment. I would walk off this plane stepping into a new world with a new beginning, a new life and a new walk.

Chapter 1 – D-Day

1. According to the author, what caused the Liberian Civil War?
2. What are the tribes of the author's ma and pa?
3. Who was the President of Liberia at the start of the war and what was his tribe?
4. What year did the Liberian Civil War begin?
5. How did the author and his family celebrate Christmas?
6. Which suburb did the author and his family live in? What was the name of his neighborhood?
7. What interesting fact did the author share about his sixth grade classmates?

Chapter 2 – Apocalypse

1. List some of the things that were strange about the appearance of the rebel soldiers.
2. Why were the rebels killing people?
3. When the author and his family stopped for a drink, what was floating in the water?
4. Describe the atmosphere inside the factory where the author and his group slept for the night.
5. The author witnessed his first, up-close killing at the Voice of America (VOA) gate. How did the killing happen? How did the author feel in that moment?

Chapter 3 – Mirage

1. The author reunites with his ma and she describes her experience while trying to find her family. What detail did she share that "amazed" the author?
2. In this chapter, we are first introduced to what will become the author's favorite pastime. Why did the author first start fishing and how did he do it?
3. What was the name of the author's first love? How old was she?

4. Why did the author and his family leave VOA?
5. What happened to pa at the conclusion of this chapter?
6. In your opinion, why was this chapter entitled "Mirage"?

Chapter 4 – The Journey

1. What were the author's thoughts about the possibility of he and his brothers joining the rebels?
2. In this chapter, the author describes being assaulted by rebel soldiers on two separate occasions. What were the circumstances under which he was hit?
3. A staple in Liberian culture and in the author's upbringing is working together and the sharing of resources amongst family and community members. How were meal times arranged to ensure equity?
4. Place yourself in the position of Esther during her interaction with the rebel soldier in the village, how would you feel? What, if anything, does this exchange tell you about the societal view of women?

Chapter 5 – Born Again

1. What was the name of the city where the author lived in this chapter? What was "ironic" about the people who lived in the new city?
2. Throughout the book, the author talked about the challenge of having adequate food and water. Describe how a nearby tree served as a highly sought after source of food for the housemates.
3. Being raised by a Christian ma and a Muslim pa, the author explained that he never had a personal connection with either religion. In this chapter, something changed. How does the author describe his "Born Again" experience?
4. What was the name of the group that pushed the rebels (NPFL) out of Monrovia?

5. Why did the author's father leave to go to the Ivory Coast?
6. The author learned that his own relatives joined the rebels. Describe how he was torn in his feelings about their decisions and subsequent actions.
7. Why did the author feel like the United States should have intervened in the Liberian Civil War?

Chapter 6 – The Expedition

1. The author and his family traveled through Gbarnga, the capital of Bong County. What detail did the driver share about the city?
2. In Kenema, what organization assisted refugees with food?
3. Throughout this chapter, the reader got a glimpse into a different way of life than that experienced in America. Discuss some of the differences (e.g., transportation, infrastructure, fueling, food, communication, etc.).
4. The author's expedition took him over land, water and even up a mountain! Which four countries did he cross?

Chapter 7 – The Village

1. What was the name of pa's village?
2. How did the villagers celebrate the arrival of the author and his family?
3. What language did the villagers speak?
4. Why did the author describe living in the village as being one of the best times of his life?
5. According to the author, why did pa say that it was good to marry a relative?
6. How was the Revolutionary United Front (RUF) similar to the National Patriotic Front of Liberia (NPFL)?

Chapter 8 - The Voyage

1. How did ma humiliate the author while in Bo?
2. What was the rude landlord's belief about Liberian refugees?
3. Who came to the aid of the author and his family in Freetown? What information did he share?
4. Where did the author and his family sleep while at the port?
5. How does the author describe his voyage from Sierra Leone to Liberia?

Chapter 9 - Home Again

1. How did the author describe the condition of Liberia upon his return?
2. Imagine yourself as the author. Describe your feelings upon returning to your home for the first time since the war began.
3. In this chapter, the author and his brother Curtis learned how to catch crabs. What traumatic event happened while they were crabbing?
4. What did the author's family do to combat the food and water crises?
5. Describe the author's near-death experience.
6. With the extra income coming in from the newly opened family drugstore, the author was able to return to school. At age thirteen, what grade did the author repeat?
7. Why was the author's brother Opa beaten by the ECOMOG soldiers?
8. While looking for rattan with his brothers in the jungle, what was it that triggered déjà vu for the author?

Chapter 10 - October Octopus

1. Why did the author believe that the operation launched by the rebels (NPFL) on the capital city, Monrovia, was called "October Octopus"?
2. Why were the ECOMOG soldiers surprised to see the author and his family leaving their neighborhood?
3. What was ironic about the location of the house where the author and his family sought refuge in Monrovia?
4. How did the author describe the ECOMOG airstrike?
5. Up until this day, the author does not drink alcohol. Describe his first drinking experience and how this may have played a role in his decision.
6. While visiting his house, the author was caught in a crossfire between the ECOMOG and rebel soldiers that he described as being his closest brush with death yet. While he did not have his "last" breath there, this day did represent a "last" for him. Explain why.
7. At the conclusion of this chapter, what analogy did the author use to describe war?

Chapter 11 - Vagabond

1. Where did the author and his family move to during the opening of this chapter?
2. What were the author's beliefs about drug use and the selling of medication?
3. Why did the author and pa return to Sierra Leone?
4. What were some of the author's beliefs about life in America? What or who had influenced his opinion?
5. How did the author describe his experience holding a gun for the first time?
6. How did pa ensure that he had enough bribe money for both the government and the rebel soldiers?

7. Again, the author sheds light on arranged marriages. What was the customary practice, described in this chapter, to prove that a new bride was a virgin on her wedding night?

8. The author made a new group of friends that he referred to as the "pack". How did he gain their respect?

9. In this chapter and throughout the book, the reader is exposed to significant differences in child-rearing practices compared to that of American culture. Discuss some of those differences.

Chapter 12 - Alone

1. What prompted the soldiers on board the truck to shoot into the jungle?

2. Although hungry, the author made a decision to share his bread with his fellow travelers. How did this benefit him later?

3. Describe the road conditions and its impact on the author.

4. What was ma's reaction to the author traveling alone?

Chapter 13 – The Audition

1. Where did the author have to move in order to qualify for the resettlement program? Why didn't the entire family move?

2. How did the author describe his first flight experience?

3. What were the author's preconceived notions about the camp? How were they disproved?

4. This is the first interaction that the reader had with the author's older brother Francis. What were some of the things that the author revealed about him?

5. Why did the author think that the other families were more qualified to go to America?

6. Describe the author's reaction to having an up close encounter with a white person.

7. Why did Francis not qualify for the resettlement program?

Chapter 14 – New World

1. According to the author, what was the significance of football (soccer) to the Liberian people?
2. The second interview for the resettlement program went better than the author expected. What did the worker advise as next steps for the author and his family?
3. What was Daddy Boy's initial reaction to the news that the author was moving to America?
4. How did the author describe the atmosphere at the camp on the day of their departure?
5. The author revealed to the reader that he was tired of living in secret. What was his secret and how did he think that America would help?
6. In what ways was the author introduced to a new world inside of the airport?
7. Aside from the fact that the author literally walked what felt like millions of miles over his lifetime, describe what you believe to be the symbolism of the book's title.
8. The author concludes the book very optimistic about what life in America will mean for him. Thinking of his walk to come, what are some of the positive outcomes that you foresee and what are some of the challenges?

   You'll have to read the next book to get the definitive answer!

Thanks for your support!
www.wlbNC.com

Made in the USA
Middletown, DE
23 April 2021